Learning React

Kirupa Chinnathambi

✦✦Addison-Wesley

Boston • Columbus • Indianapolis • New York • San Francisco • Amsterdam • Cape Town
Dubai • London • Madrid • Milan • Munich • Paris • Montreal • Toronto • Delhi
Mexico City • Sao Paulo • Sidney • Hong Kong • Seoul • Singapore • Taipei • Tokyo

Learning React

ISBN-13: 978-0-134-54631-5

ISBN-10: 0-134-54631-8

Library of Congress Control Number: 2016917161

Printed in the United States of America

1   16

Trademarks

Warning and Disclaimer

Special Sales

For information about buying this title in bulk quantities, or for special sales opportunities (which may include electronic versions; custom cover designs; and content particular to your business, training goals, marketing focus, or branding interests), please contact our corporate sales department at corpsales@pearsoned.com or (800) 382-3419.

For government sales inquiries, please contact governmentsales@pearsoned.com.

For questions about sales outside the United States, please contact intlcs@pearsoned.com.

Acquisitions Editor
Mark Taber

Development Editor
Chris Zahn

Copy Editor
Abigail Manheim

Indexer
Erika Millen

Technical Reviewers
Trevor McCauley
Kyle Murray

Cover Designer
Chuti Prasertsith

Accessing the Free Web Edition

Your purchase of this book in any format includes access to the corresponding Web Edition, which provides several special online-only features:

- The complete text of the book
- Bonus material on animating content with React Motion and making Ajax/server-related calls
- Updates and corrections as they become available

The Web Edition can be viewed on all types of computers and mobile devices with any modern web browser that supports HTML5.

To get access to the *Learning React* Web Edition all you need to do is register this book:

1. Go to www.informit.com/register
2. Sign in or create a new account.
3. Enter ISBN: **9780134546315**
4. Answer the questions as proof of purchase.
5. The Web Edition will appear under the Digital Purchases tab on your Account page. Click the Launch link to access the product.

❖

To my dad!

*(Who always believed in me—even if what I was often doing
made no sense to him...or to me for that matter! :P)*

❖

Contents

Acknowledgments

First, none of this would be possible without the support and encouragement of my awesome wife, **Meena**. If she didn't put her goals on hold to allow me to spend six months designing, writing, and re-writing everything you see here, me writing this book would have been a distant dream.

Next, I'd like to thank **my parents** for always encouraging me to aimlessly wander and enjoy free time to do what I liked—such as teaching complete strangers over the internet in the late 1990s how to do cool things with programming. I wouldn't be half the rugged indoorsman/scholar/warrior I am today without them both :P

On the publishing side, writing the words you see here is the easy part. Getting the book into your hands is an amazingly complex process. The more I learn about all the moving pieces involved, the more impressed I am at all the individuals who work tirelessly behind the scenes to keep this amazing machinery running. **To everyone at Pearson** who made this possible, thank you! There are a few people I'd like to explicitly call out, though. First, I'd like to thank **Mark Taber** for continuing to give me opportunities to work together, **Chris Zahn** for patiently addressing my numerous questions/concerns, **Abby Manheim** for turning my version of English into something human-understandable, and **Loretta Yates** for helping make the connections a long time ago that made all of this happen. The technical content of this book has been reviewed in great detail by my long-time friends and online collaborators, **Kyle Murray (aka Krilnon)** and **Trevor McCauley (aka senocular)**. I can't thank them enough for their thorough (and frequently, humorous!) feedback.

About the Author

Kirupa Chinnathambi has spent most of his life trying to teach others to love web development as much as he does.

In 1999, before blogging was even a word, he started posting tutorials on kirupa.com. In the years since then, he has written hundreds of articles, written a few books (none as good as this one, of course!), and recorded a bunch of videos you can find on YouTube. When he isn't writing or talking about web development, he spends his waking hours helping make the Web more awesome as a Program Manager in Microsoft. In his non-waking hours, he is probably sleeping...or writing about himself in the third person.

You can find him on Twitter (twitter.com/kirupa), Facebook (facebook.com/kirupa), or e-mail (kirupa@kirupa.com). Feel free to contact him anytime.

Introducing React

Ignoring for a moment that web apps today both *look* and *feel* nicer than they did back in the day, there is something even more fundamental that has changed. The way we architect and build web apps is very different now. To highlight this, let's take a look at the app shown in Figure 1-1.

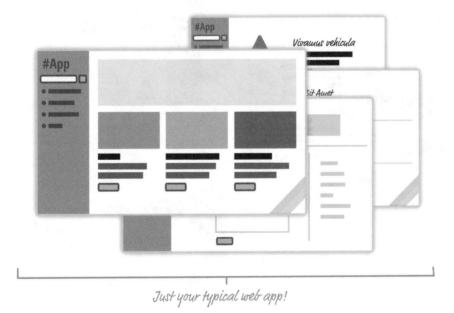

Just your typical web app!

Figure 1-1   An app.

This app is a simple catalog browser for something. Like any app of this sort, you have your usual set of pages revolving around a home page, a search results page, a details page, and so on. In the following sections, let's look at the two approaches we have for building this app. Yes, in some mysterious fashion, this leads to us getting an overview of React as well!

Onwards!

Old School Multi-Page Design

If you had to build this app a few years ago, you may have taken an approach that involved multiple, individual pages. The flow would have looked something like what is shown in Figure 1-2.

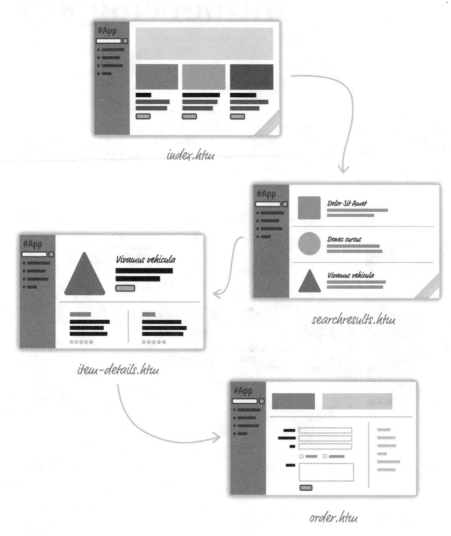

Figure 1-2   Multi-page design.

For almost every action that changes what the browser displays, the web app will navigate you to a *whole different page*. This is a big deal beyond the less-than-stellar user experience that users will see as pages get torn down and redrawn. This has a big impact on how you maintain your app state. Outside of storing some user data via cookies and some server-side mechanism, you simply don't need to care. Life is good.

New School Single-Page Apps

Today, going with a web app model that requires navigating between individual pages seems dated...like, really dated, like what is shown in Figure 1-3.

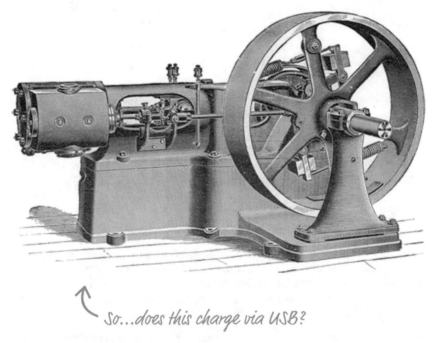

So...does this charge via USB?

Figure 1-3   The individual page model is a bit dated—like this steam engine.
Source: *New Catechism of the Steam Engine*, 1904

Instead, modern apps tend to adhere to what is known as a **Single-page app (SPA) model**. This is a world where you never navigate to different pages or ever even reload a page. Instead, the different views of your app are loaded and unloaded into the same page itself.

For our app, this may look something like Figure 1-4.

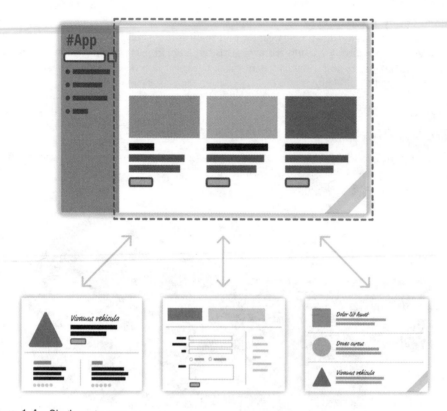

Figure 1-4   Single-page app.

As users interact with our app, we replace the contents of the dotted red region with the data and HTML that matches what the user is trying to do. The end result is a much more fluid experience. You can even use a lot of visual techniques to have your new content transition in nicely just like you might see in cool apps on your mobile device or desktop. This sort of stuff is simply not possible when navigating to different pages.

All of this may sound a bit crazy if you've never heard of single-page apps before, but there is a very good chance you've run into some of them in the wild. If you've ever used popular web apps like Gmail, Facebook, Instagram, or Twitter, you were using a single-page app. In all those apps, the content gets dynamically displayed without requiring you to refresh or navigate to a different page.

Now, I am making these single-page apps seem really complicated. That's not *entirely* the case. Thanks to a lot of great improvements in both JavaScript and a variety of third party frameworks and libraries, building single-page apps has never been easier. That doesn't mean there is no room for improvement, though.

When building single-page apps, there are three major issues that you'll encounter:

- **In a single-page application, the bulk of your time will be spent keeping your data in sync with your UI.** For example, if a user loads new content, do we explicitly clear out the search field? Do we keep the active tab on a navigation element still visible? Which elements do we keep on the page, and which do we destroy?

  These are all problems unique to single-page apps. When navigating between pages in the old model, we just assumed everything in our UI would be destroyed and just built back up again. This was never a problem.

- **Manipulating the DOM is really REALLY slow.** Manually querying elements, adding children (see Figure 1-5 below), removing subtrees, and performing other DOM operations are some of the slowest things you can do in your browser. Unfortunately, in a single-page app, you'll be doing a lot of this. Manipulating the DOM is the primary way you are able to respond to user actions and display new content.

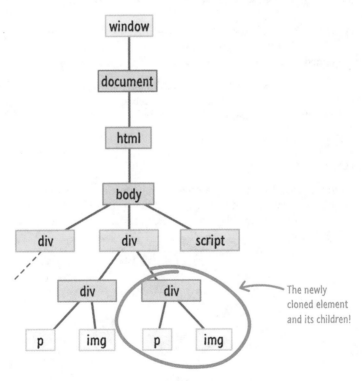

Figure 1-5   Adding children.

- **Working with HTML templates can be a pain.** Navigation in a single-page app is nothing more than you dealing with fragments of HTML to represent whatever it is you wish to display. These fragments of HTML are often known as **templates**, and using JavaScript to manipulate them and fill them out with data gets really complicated really quickly.

To make things worse, depending on the framework you are using, the way your templates look and interact with data can vary wildly. For example, this is what using a template in Mustache looks like:

```javascript
var view = {
  title: "Joe",
  calc: function () {
    return 2 + 4;
  }
};

var output = Mustache.render("{{title}} spends {{calc}}", view);
```

Sometimes, your templates may look like some clean HTML that you can proudly show off in front of the class. Other times, your templates might be unintelligible, with a boatload of custom tags designed to help map your HTML elements to some data.

Despite these shortcomings, single-page apps aren't going anywhere. They are a part of the present, and they will fully form the future of how web apps are built. That doesn't mean that we have to tolerate these shortcomings. To address this, meet React!

Meet React

Facebook (and Instagram) decided that enough is enough. Given their abundance of experience with single-page apps, they released a library called **React** (the React logo is shown in Figure 1-6) to not only address these shortcomings, but to also change how we think about building single-page apps.

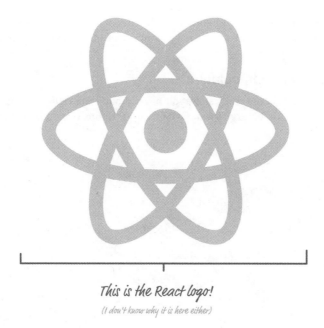

This is the React logo!

(I don't know why it is here either.)

Figure 1-6   The React logo.

In the following sections, let's look at the big things React brings to the table.

Automatic UI State Management

With single-page apps, keeping track of your UI and maintaining state is hard—and very time-consuming. With React, you need to worry only about one thing: *the final state your UI is in*. It doesn't matter what state your UI started out in. It doesn't matter what series of steps your users may have taken to change the UI. All that matters is where your UI ended up (see Figure 1-7).

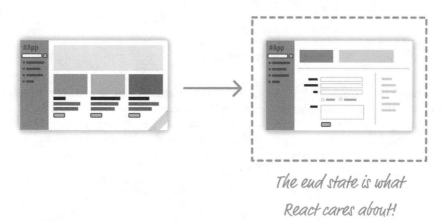

The end state is what React cares about!

Figure 1-7   The final or end state of your UI is what matters in React.

React takes care of everything else. It figures out what needs to happen to ensure your UI is represented properly, so all of that state management stuff is no longer your concern.

Lightning-fast DOM Manipulation

Because DOM modifications are really slow, you never modify the DOM directly using React. Instead, you modify an in-memory *virtual* DOM instead. Figure 1-8 symbolizes that in-memory virtual DOM.

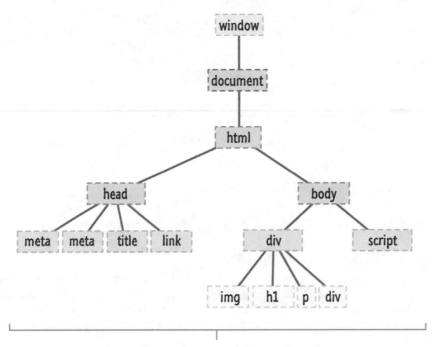

The virtual DOM looks nothing like this. It is also not going to be this colorful :(

Figure 1-8   Imagine an in-memory virtual DOM.

Manipulating this virtual DOM is extremely fast, and React takes care of updating the real DOM when the time is right. It does so by comparing the changes between your virtual DOM and the real DOM, figuring out which changes actually matter, and making the least amount of DOM changes needed to keep everything up-to-date in a process called **reconciliation**.

APIs to Create Truly Composable UIs

Instead of treating the visual elements in your app as one monolithic chunk, React encourages you to break your visual elements into smaller and smaller components.

Just like everything else in programming, it is a good idea to have things be modular, compact, and self-contained. React extends that well-established idea to how we should think about user interfaces as well. Many of React's core APIs make it easier to create smaller visual components that can later be combined with other visual components to make larger and more complex visual components—kind of like Russian Matryoshka dolls (see Figure 1-9).

Figure 1-9   Russian Matryoshka dolls by Gnomz007.
Source: *https://commons.wikimedia.org/wiki/File:Russian-Matroshka_no_bg.jpg*

This is one of the major ways React simplifies (and changes) how we think about building the visuals for our web apps.

Visuals Defined Entirely in JavaScript

While this sounds ridiculously crazy and outrageous, hear me out. Besides using a really weird syntax, HTML templates traditionally suffered from another major problem. The variety of things you can do inside them other than simply displaying data is limited. If you wanted to choose which piece of UI to display based on a particular condition, for example, you had to write JavaScript somewhere else in your app or use some weird framework-specific templating command to make it work.

For example, here is what a conditional statement inside an EmberJS template looks like:

```
{{#if person}}
  Welcome back, <b>{{person.firstName}} {{person.lastName}}</b>!
{{else}}
  Please log in.
{{/if}}
```

What React does is pretty neat. By having your UI defined entirely in JavaScript, you get to use all of the rich functionality JavaScript provides for doing all sorts of things inside your templates (as you will see in a few chapters). You are limited only by what JavaScript supports as opposed to any limitations imposed by your templating framework.

Now, when you think of visuals defined entirely in JavaScript, you are probably thinking something horrible involving quotation marks, escape characters, and a whole lot of createEle-ment calls. Don't worry. React gives you the option to specify your visuals using an HTML-like syntax known as **JSX** that lives fully alongside your JavaScript. Instead of writing code to define your UI, you are basically specifying markup:

```
ReactDOM.render(
  <div>
    <h1>Batman</h1>
    <h1>Iron Man</h1>
    <h1>Nicolas Cage</h1>
    <h1>Mega Man</h1>
  </div>,
  destination
);
```

This same code defined in JavaScript would look like this:

```
ReactDOM.render(React.createElement(
  "div",
  null,
  React.createElement(
    "h1",
    null,
    "Batman"
  ),
  React.createElement(
    "h1",
    null,
    "Iron Man"
  ),
  React.createElement(
    "h1",
    null,
    "Nicolas Cage"
  ),
```

```
React.createElement(
    "h1",
    null,
    "Mega Man"
  )
), destination);
```

Yikes! By using JSX, you are able to define your visuals very easily using a syntax that is very familiar, while still getting all the power and flexibility that JavaScript provides. Best of all, in React, your visuals and JavaScript often live in the same location. You no longer have to jump between multiple files to define the look and behavior of one visual component. This is templating done right.

Just the V in an MVC Architecture

We are almost done here! React is not a full-fledged framework that has an opinion on how everything in your app should behave. Instead, React works primarily in the View layer where all of its worries and concerns revolve around your visual elements and keeping them up to date. This means you are free to use whatever you want for the M and C part of your MVC architecture. This flexibility enables you to pick and choose what technologies you are familiar with, and this makes React useful not only for new web apps you create but also for existing apps you'd like to enhance without removing and refactoring a whole bunch of code.

Conclusion

As new web frameworks and libraries go, React is quite the runaway success. It not only deals with the most common problems developers faced when building single-page apps, it throws in a few additional tricks that make building the visuals for your single-page apps much MUCH easier. Since it came out in 2013, React has steadily found its way into popular web sites and apps that you probably use. Besides Facebook and Instagram, some of the notable ones include the BBC, Khan Academy, PayPal, Reddit, The New York Times, Yahoo, and many more: https://github.com/facebook/react/wiki/Sites-Using-React

The intent of this chapter is to provide you with an introduction to what React does and why it does it. In tutorials in subsequent chapters we'll dive deeper into everything you've seen here and cover the technical details that will help you successfully use React in your own projects. Stick around.

2

Building Your First React App

By now, thanks to the previous chapter, you probably know all about the backstory of React and how it helps even your most complex user interfaces sing performantly. For all the awesomeness that React brings to the table, getting started with it (kinda like this sentence) is not the most straightforward thing. It has a steep learning curve filled with many small and big hurdles:

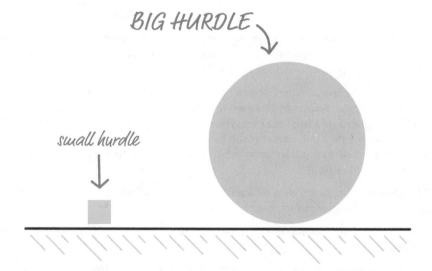

In this chapter, we start at the very beginning and get our hands dirty by building a simple React app. We encounter some of these hurdles head-on, and some of these hurdles we skip over—for now. By the end of this chapter, not only will we have built something you can proudly show off to your friends and family, we'll have set ourselves up nicely for diving deeper into all that React offers in future chapters.

Dealing with JSX

Before we start building our app, there is an important thing we should cover first. React isn't like many JavaScript libraries you may have used. It isn't very happy when you simply refer to code you've written for it using a script tag. React is annoyingly special that way, and it has to do with how React apps are built.

As you know, your web apps (and everything else your browser displays) are made up of HTML, CSS, and JavaScript:

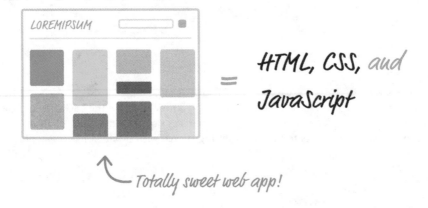

It doesn't matter if your web app was written using React or some other library like Angular, Knockout, or jQuery. *The end result* has to be some combination of HTML, CSS, and JavaScript. Otherwise, your browser really won't know what to do.

Now, here is where the special nature of React comes in. *Besides normal HTML, CSS, and JavaScript, the bulk of your React code will be written in something known as JSX.* JSX, as I mentioned in Chapter 1, is a language that allows you to easily mix JavaScript and HTML-like tags to define user interface (UI) elements and their functionality. That sounds cool and all (and we will see JSX in action in just a few moments), but there is a slight problem. Your browser has no idea what to do with JSX.

To build a web app using React, we need a way to take our JSX and convert it into plain old JavaScript that your browser can understand.

If we didn't do this, our React app simply wouldn't work. That's not cool. Fortunately, there are two solutions to this:

- **Set up a development environment around Node and a handful of build-tools.** In this environment, every time you perform a build, all of your JSX is automatically converted into JS and placed on disk for you to reference like any plain JavaScript file.

- **Let your browser rely on a JavaScript library to automatically convert JSX to something it understands.** You specify your JSX directly just like you would any old piece of JavaScript, and your browser takes care of the rest.

Both of these solutions have a place in our world, but let's talk about the impact of each.

The first solution, while a bit complicated and time-consuming at first, is *the way* modern web development is done these days. Besides compiling (transpiling to be more accurate) your JSX to JS, this approach enables you to take advantage of modules, better build tools, and a bunch of other features that make building complex web apps somewhat manageable.

The second solution provides a quick and direct path where you initially spend more time writing code and less time fiddling with your development environment. To use this solution, all you do is reference a script file. This script file takes care of turning the JSX into JS on page load, and your React app comes to life without you having to do anything special to your development environment.

For our introductory look at React, we are going to use the second solution. You may be wondering why we don't use the second solution always. The reason is that your browser takes a performance hit each time it spends time translating JSX into JS. That is totally acceptable when learning how to use React, but that is totally not acceptable when deploying your app for real-life use. Because of that un-acceptableness, we will revisit all of this and look at the first solution and how to set up your development environment later, once you've gotten your feet comfortably wet in React.

Getting Your React On

In the previous section, we looked at the two ways you have for ensuring your React app ends up as something your browser understands. In this section, we are going to put all of those words into practice. First, we will need a blank HTML page that will act as our starting point.

If you don't have a blank HTML page handy, feel free to use the following:

```
<!DOCTYPE html>
<html>

<head>
  <title>React! React! React!</title>
</head>

<body>
  <script>

  </script>
</body>

</html>
```

This page has nothing interesting or exciting going for it, but let's fix that by adding a reference to the React library. Just below the `title`, add these two lines:

```
<script src="https://unpkg.com/react@15.3.2/dist/react.js"></script>
<script src="https://unpkg.com/react-dom@15.3.2/dist/react-dom.js"></script>
```

These two lines bring in both the core React library as well as the various things React needs to work with the DOM. Without them, you aren't building a React app at all. Now, we aren't done yet. There is one more library we need to reference. Just below these two `script` tags, add the following line:

```
<script src="https://cdnjs.cloudflare.com/ajax/libs/babel-core/5.8.23/browser.min.
js"></script>
```

What we are doing here is adding a reference to the Babel JavaScript compiler (http://babeljs .io/). Babel does many cool things, but the one we care about is its capability to turn JSX into JavaScript.

At this point, our HTML page should look as follows:

```
<!DOCTYPE html>
<html>

<head>
  <title>React! React! React!</title>
  <script src="https://unpkg.com/react@15.3.2/dist/react.js"></script>
  <script src="https://unpkg.com/react-dom@15.3.2/dist/react-dom.js"></script>
  <script src="https://cdnjs.cloudflare.com/ajax/libs/babel-core/5.8.23/browser.min.
js"></script>
</head>

<body>
  <script>

  </script>
</body>

</html>
```

If you preview your page right now, you'll notice that this page is still blank with nothing visible going on. That's OK. We are going to fix that next.

Displaying Your Name

The first thing we are going to do is use React to display our name on screen. The way we do that is by using a method called `render`. Inside your `script` tag, add the following:

```
ReactDOM.render(
  <h1>Sherlock Holmes</h1>,
  document.body
);
```

Don't worry if none of this makes sense at this point. Our goal is to get something to display on screen first, and we'll make sense of what we did shortly afterwards. Now, before we preview this in our page to see what happens, we need to designate this `script` block as something that Babel can do its magic on. The way we do that is by setting the `type` attribute on the script tag to a value of `text/babel`:

```
<script type="text/babel">
  ReactDOM.render(
    <h1>Sherlock Holmes</h1>,
    document.body
  );
</script>
```

Once you've made that change, now preview what you have in your browser. What you'll see are the words **Sherlock Holmes** printed in giant letters. Congratulations! You just built an app using React.

As apps go, this isn't all that exciting. Chances are your name isn't even Sherlock Holmes. While this app doesn't have much going for it, it does introduce you to one of the most frequently used methods you'll use in the React universe—the `ReactDOM.render` method.

The `render` method takes two arguments:

- The HTML-like elements (aka JSX) you wish to output
- The location in the DOM that React will render the JSX into

Here is what our render method looks like:

```
ReactDOM.render(
  <h1>Sherlock Holmes</h1>,
  document.body
);
```

Our first argument is the text **Sherlock Holmes** wrapped inside some h1 tags. This HTML-like syntax inside your JavaScript is what JSX is all about. While we will spend a lot more time drilling into JSX a bit later, I should mention this up front—*It is every bit as crazy as it looks*. Whenever I see brackets and slashes in JavaScript, a part of me dies on the inside because of all the string escaping and quotation mark gibberish I will need to do. With JSX, you do none of that. You just place your HTML-like content as-is just like what we've done here. Magically (like the super-awesome kind involving dragons and laser beams), it all works.

The second argument is `document.body`. There is nothing crazy or bizarre about this argument. It simply specifies where the converted markup from the JSX will end up living in our DOM. In our example, when the `render` method runs, the h1 tag (and everything inside it) is placed in our document's body element.

Now, the goal of this exercise wasn't to display *a* name on the screen. It was to display *your* name. Go ahead and modify your code to do that. In my case, the `render` method will look as follows:

```
ReactDOM.render(
  <h1>Batman</h1>,
  document.body
);
```

Well—it would look like that if my name was Batman! Anyway, if you preview your page now, you will see your name displayed instead of Sherlock Holmes.

It's All Still Familiar

While the JavaScript looks new and shiny thanks to JSX, the end result your browser sees is nice, clean HTML, CSS, and JavaScript. To see this for yourself, let's make a few alterations to how our app behaves and looks.

Changing the Destination

The first thing we'll do is change where our JSX gets output. Using JavaScript to place things directly in your body element is never a good idea. A lot can go wrong—especially if you are going to be mixing React with other JS libraries and frameworks. The recommended path is to create a separate element that you will treat as a new root element. This element will serve as the destination our render method will use. To make this happen, go back to the HTML and add a div element with an id value of container.

Instead of showing you the full HTML for this one minor change, here is what just our body element looks like:

```
<body>
  <div id="container"></div>
  <script type="text/babel">
    ReactDOM.render(
      <h1>Batman</h1>,
      document.body
    );
  </script>
</body>
```

With our **container** div element safely defined, let's modify the render method to use it instead of document.body. Here is one way of doing this:

```
ReactDOM.render(
  <h1>Batman</h1>,
  document.querySelector("#container")
);
```

Another way of doing this is by doing some things outside of the render method itself:

```
var destination = document.querySelector("#container");

ReactDOM.render(
  <h1>Batman</h1>,
  destination
);
```

Notice that the `destination` variable stores the reference to our container DOM element. Inside the `render` method, we simply reference the same `destination` variable instead of writing the full element-finding syntax as part of the argument itself. The reason I want to do this is simple. I want to show you that you are still writing JavaScript and `render` is just another boring old method that happens to take two arguments.

Styling It Up!

Time for our last change before we call it a day. Right now, our names show up in whatever default `h1` styling our browser provides. That is just terrible, so let's fix it by adding some CSS. Inside your `head` tag, add a `style` block with the following CSS:

```
#container {
  padding: 50px;
  background-color: #EEE;
}
#container h1 {
  font-size: 48px;
  font-family: sans-serif;
  color: #0080A8;
}
```

After you have added all of this, preview your page. Notice that our text appears with a little more purpose than it did earlier when it relied entirely on the browser's default styling (see Figure 2-1).

Figure 2-1   The result of adding the CSS.

The reason this works is that our DOM's body, after running all of the React code, contains our **container** element with an h1 tag inside it. It doesn't matter that the h1 tag was defined entirely inside JavaScript in this JSX syntax or that your CSS was defined well outside of the render method. The end result is that your React app is still going to be made up of some 100% organic (and cage-free!) HTML, CSS, and JavaScript:

```
<!DOCTYPE html>
<html>

<head>
  <title>React! React! React!</title>
  <script src="https://unpkg.com/react@15.3.2/dist/react.js"></script>
  <script src="https://unpkg.com/react-dom@15.3.2/dist/react-dom.js"></script>
  <script src="https://cdnjs.cloudflare.com/ajax/libs/babel-core/5.8.23/browser.min.js"></script>

  <style>
    #container {
      padding: 50px;
      background-color: #EEE;
    }
    #container h1 {
      font-size: 144px;
      font-family: sans-serif;
      color: #0080a8;
    }
  </style>
</head>

<body>
  <div id="container"></div>
  <script type="text/babel">
    var destination = document.querySelector("#container");

    ReactDOM.render(React.createElement(
      "h1",
      null,
      "Batman"
    ), destination);
  </script>
</body>

</html>
```

Notice that there is nary a trace of React-like code in sight. Also, we should use the word *nary* more often in everyday conversation!

Conclusion

If this is your first time building a React app, we covered a lot of ground here. One of the biggest takeaways is that React is different than other libraries because it uses a whole new language called JSX to define what the visuals will look like. We got a very small glimpse of that here when we defined the `h1` tag inside the `render` method.

JSX's impact goes beyond how you define your UI elements. It also alters how you build your app as a whole. Because your browser can't understand JSX in its native representation, you need to use an intermediate step to convert that JSX into JavaScript. One approach is to build your app to generate the transpiled JavaScript output to correspond to the JSX source. Another approach (aka the one we used here) is to use the Babel library to translate the JSX into JavaScript on the browser itself. While the performance hit of doing that is not recommended for live/production apps, when familiarizing yourself with React, you can't beat the convenience.

In future chapters, we'll spend some time diving deeper into JSX and going beyond the render method as we look at all the important things that make React tick.

3

Components in React

Components are one of the things that make React, well, React! They are one of the primary ways you have for defining the visuals and interactions that make up what people see when they use your app. Let's say Figure 3-1 shows what your finished app looks like.

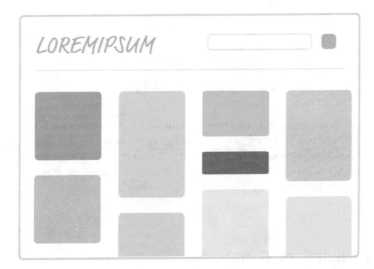

Figure 3-1   Your hypothetical finished app.

This is the finished sausage. During development, viewed from the lens of you as a React developer, things might look a little less appealing. Almost every part of this app's visuals would be wrapped inside a self-contained module known as a **component**. To highlight what "almost every" means here, take a look at the diagram in Figure 3-2.

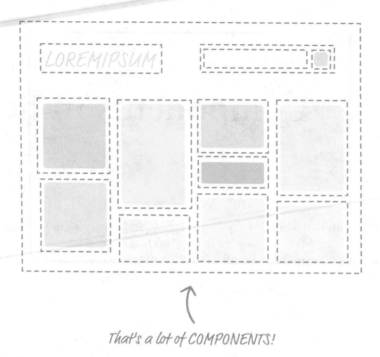

That's a lot of COMPONENTS!

Figure 3-2   Diagrammatic representation of the app components.

Each dotted line represents an individual component that is responsible for both what you see as well as any interactions that it may be responsible for. Don't let this scare you. While this looks really complicated, as you will see shortly, it will start to make a whole lot of sense once you've had a chance to play with components and some of the awesome things that they do—or at least try really hard to do.

Onwards!

A Quick Review of Functions

In JavaScript, you have these things known as **functions**. They enable you to make your code a bit cleaner and more reusable. Now, there is reason why we are taking some time to look at functions, and it isn't to annoy you—I swear! Functions, conceptually speaking, share a lot of surface area with React components, and the easiest way to understand what components do is by taking a quick look at functions first.

In a terrible world where functions do not exist, you may have some code that looks as follows:

```
var speed = 10;
var time = 5;
alert(speed * time);
```

```
var speed1 = 85;
var time1 = 1.5;
alert(speed1 * time1);

var speed2 = 12;
var time2 = 9;
alert(speed2 * time2);

var speed3 = 42;
var time3 = 21;
alert(speed3 * time3);
```

In a really chill world that involves functions, you can condense all of that duplicated text into something simple like the following:

```
function getDistance(speed, time) {
    var result = speed * time;
    alert(result);
}
```

Our getDistance function removes all of the duplicated code you saw earlier, and it takes speed and time as arguments to enable you to customize the calculation that gets returned.

To call this function, all you have to do is this:

```
getDistance(10, 5);
getDistance(85, 1.5);
getDistance(12, 9);
getDistance(42, 21);
```

Doesn't this look nicer? Now there is another great value functions provide. Your functions (like the alert inside getDistance) can call other functions as part of their running. Here is us using a formatDistance function to change what gets returned by getDistance:

```
1  function formatDistance(distance) {
2      return distance + "km";
3  }
4
5  function getDistance(speed, time) {
6      var result = speed * time;
7      alert(formatDistance(result));
8  }
```

This capability to have functions call other functions enables us to cleanly separate what functions do. You don't need to have one monolithic function that does everything under the sun. You can distribute the functionality across many functions specialized for a particular type of task.

Best of all, after you make changes to how your functions work, you don't have to do anything extra to see the results of those changes. If the function signature did not change, any existing calls to that function will just magically work and automatically pick up any new changes you made to the function itself. For example, our existing `getDistance` calls will see the result of the `formatDistance` function even if the `formatDistance` function didn't exist when the calls were first defined. That's pretty awesome.

In a nutshell, functions are awesome. I know that. You know that. That's why all of the code we write has them all over the place.

Changing How We Deal with the UI

I don't think anybody will disagree with the good things functions bring to the table. They really make it possible to structure the code for your apps in a sane way. That same level of care we use in writing our code isn't always possible when it comes to writing our UIs. For various technical and non-technical reasons, we've always tolerated a certain level of sloppiness with how we typically work with our UI elements.

I realize that is a pretty controversial statement, so let me highlight what I mean by looking at some examples. We are going to go back and look at the `render` method we used in the previous chapter:

```
var destination = document.querySelector("#container");

ReactDOM.render(
  <h1>Batman</h1>,
  destination
);
```

What you see on the screen is the word **Batman** printed in giant letters—thanks to the `h1` element. Let's change things up a bit and say that we want to print the names of several other superheroes. To do this, let's modify our `render` method to now look as follows:

```
var destination = document.querySelector("#container");

ReactDOM.render(
  <div>
    <h1>Batman</h1>
    <h1>Iron Man</h1>
    <h1>Nicolas Cage</h1>
    <h1>Mega Man</h1>
  </div>,
  destination
);
```

Notice what you see here. We emit a `div` that contains the four `h1` elements with our superhero names.

JSX Gotcha: Outputting Multiple Elements

There is an important JSX detail to call out here. The `div` that wraps our `h1` elements isn't there because it looks like a good idea. It is there because it *has to be there*. In React, you can't output multiple adjacent elements as shown in the following:

```
var destination = document.querySelector("#container");

ReactDOM.render(
  <h1>Batman</h1>
  <h1>Iron Man</h1>
  <h1>Nicolas Cage</h1>
  <h1>Mega Man</h1>,
  destination
);
```

Even though this is valid HTML, it isn't valid in the eyes of the unholy alliance between JSX and JavaScript. That may sound like a terrible limitation, but the workaround is really easy. While you can only output *one element*, this *one element can have as many children as needed*. That is why we wrap our `h1` elements inside the `div`. We do this because of how JSX gets turned into JavaScript. The details of that are something we will look at later, but it isn't important enough right this moment to distract us from learning about components.

Ok, so what we have now are four `h1` elements that each contain the name of a superhero. What if we want to change our `h1` element to something like an `h3` instead? We can manually update all of these elements as follows:

```
var destination = document.querySelector("#container");

ReactDOM.render(
  <div>
    <h3>Batman</h3>
    <h3>Iron Man</h3>
    <h3>Nicolas Cage</h3>
    <h3>Mega Man</h3>
  </div>,
  destination
);
```

If you preview what we have, you'll see something that looks a bit unstyled and plain (see Figure 3-3).

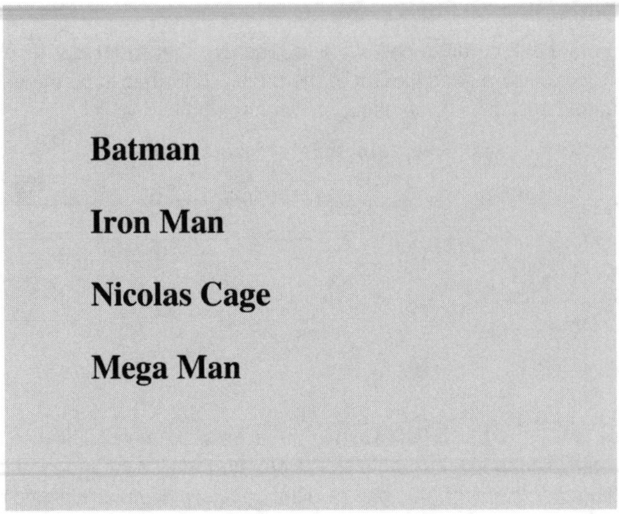

Batman

Iron Man

Nicolas Cage

Mega Man

Figure 3-3   Plain vanilla super hero names.

We don't want to go crazy with the styling here. All we want to do is just italicize all of these names by using the `<i>` tag, so let's manually update what we render by making this change:

```
var destination = document.querySelector("#container");

ReactDOM.render(
  <div>
    <h3><i>Batman</i></h3>
    <h3><i>Iron Man</i></h3>
    <h3><i>Nicolas Cage</i></h3>
    <h3><i>Mega Man</i></h3>
  </div>,
  destination
);
```

We went through each h3 element and wrapped the content inside some i tags. Can you start to see the problem here? What we are doing with our UI is no different than having code that looks as follows:

```
var speed = 10;
var time = 5;
alert(speed * time);

var speed1 = 85;
var time1 = 1.5;
alert(speed1 * time1);

var speed2 = 12;
var time2 = 9;
alert(speed2 * time2);
```

```
var speed3 = 42;
var time3 = 21;
alert(speed3 * time3);
```

Every change we want to make to our h1 or h3 elements needs to be duplicated for every instance of it. What if we want to do something even more complex than just modifying the appearance of our elements? What if we want to represent something more complex than the simple examples we are using so far? What we are doing right now won't scale because manually updating every copy of what we want to modify is time consuming. It is also boring.

Now, here is a crazy thought: What if everything awesome we looked at about functions can somehow be applied to how we define our app's visuals? Wouldn't that solve all of the inefficiencies we've highlighted in this section? Well, as it turns out, the answer to that "What if" forms the core of what React is all about. It is time for you to meet the component.

Meet the React Component

The solution to all of our problems (even the existential ones we grapple with!) can be found in React components. *React components are reusable chunks of JavaScript that output (via JSX) HTML elements.* That sounds really pedestrian for something capable of solving great problems and doing great things, but as we start to build components and gradually turn up the complexity, you'll see that components are really powerful and every bit as awesome as I've portrayed them to you.

Let's start by building a couple of components together. To follow along, start with a blank React document:

```
<!DOCTYPE html>
<html>

<head>
  <title>React Components</title>
  <script src="https://unpkg.com/react@15.3.2/dist/react.js"></script>
  <script src="https://unpkg.com/react-dom@15.3.2/dist/react-dom.js"></script>
  <script src="https://cdnjs.cloudflare.com/ajax/libs/babel-core/5.8.23/browser.min.
js"></script>
</head>

<body>
  <div id="container"></div>
  <script type="text/babel">

  </script>
</body>

</html>
```

There is nothing exciting going on this page. Nearly identical to what we had in our earlier chapter, this page is pretty barebones, with just a reference to the React and Babel libraries and a div element who proudly sports an id value of **container**.

Creating a Hello, World! Component

We are going to start really simple. What we want to do is use a component to help us print the famous "**Hello, world!**" text to the screen. As we already know, by using just the `render` method of `ReactDOM`, the code would look as follows:

```
1 | ReactDOM.render(
2 |   <div>
3 |     <p>Hello, world!</p>
4 |   </div>,
5 |   document.querySelector("#container")
6 | );
```

Let's recreate all of this by using a component. You have several ways of creating components in React, but the way we are going to create them initially is by using `React.createClass`. Go ahead and add the following highlighted code just above our existing render method:

```
var HelloWorld = React.createClass({

});


ReactDOM.render(
  <div>
    <p>Hello, world!</p>
  </div>,
  document.querySelector("#container")
);
```

What we have done is create a new component called `HelloWorld`. This `HelloWorld` component doesn't do anything right now. In fact, it is basically an empty JavaScript object at this point. Inside this object, you can put all sorts of properties to further define what `HelloWorld` does. Some properties you define are special and used by React to help your components work their magic. One such mandatory property is `render`.

Go ahead and modify our `HelloWorld` component by adding a `render` property as shown in the following:

```
var HelloWorld = React.createClass({
  render: function() {

  }
});
```

Just like the `render` method of we saw a few moments earlier as part of `ReactDOM.render`, the `render` method inside a component is also responsible for dealing with JSX. Let's modify our `render` method to return **Hello, componentized world!**, so go ahead and add the following highlighted lines:

```
var HelloWorld = React.createClass({
  render: function() {
```

```
    return (
      <p>Hello, componentized world!</p>
    );
  }
});
```

What we've done is told our `render` method to return the JSX that represents our **Hello, componentized world!** text. All that remains is to actually use this component. The way you use a component once you've defined it is by **calling** it, and we are going to call it from our old friend, the `ReactDOM.render` method:

```
ReactDOM.render(
  <HelloWorld/>,
  document.querySelector("#container")
);
```

That isn't a typo! The JSX we use for calling our `HelloWorld` component is the very HTML-like `<HelloWorld/>`. If you preview your page in your browser, you'll see the text **Hello, componentized world!** showing up on your screen. If you held your breath in suspense, you can relax.

If you have difficulty relaxing after seeing the syntax we used for calling `HelloWorld`, stare at the following circle for a few moments:

Just relax and focus on this circle!

Ok, back to reality. What we've done so far might seem crazy, but simply think of your `<HelloWorld/>` component as a cool and new HTML tag whose functionality you have full control over. This means you can do all sorts of HTML-ey things to it.

For example, go ahead and modify our `ReactDOM.render` method to look as follows:

```
ReactDOM.render(
  <div>
    <HelloWorld/>
  </div>,
  document.querySelector("#container")
);
```

We wrapped our call to the `HelloWorld` component inside a `div` element, and if you preview this in your browser, everything still works. Let's go one step further! Instead of having just a single call to `HelloWorld`, let's make a bunch of calls. Modify our `ReactDOM.render` method to now look as follows:

```
ReactDOM.render(
  <div>
    <HelloWorld/>
    <HelloWorld/>
    <HelloWorld/>
    <HelloWorld/>
    <HelloWorld/>
    <HelloWorld/>
  </div>,
  document.querySelector("#container")
);
```

What you will see now is a bunch of **Hello, componentized world!** text instances appear. Let's do one more thing before we move on to something shinier. Go back to our `HelloWorld` component declaration, and change the text we return to the more traditional **Hello, world!** value:

```
var HelloWorld = React.createClass({
  render: function() {
    return (
      <p>Hello, world!</p>
    );
  }
});
```

Just make this one change and preview your example. This time around, all of the various `HelloWorld` calls we specified earlier now return **Hello, world!** to the screen. There was no manually modifying every `HelloWorld` call. That's a good thing!

Specifying Properties

Right now, our component does just one thing. It prints **Hello, world!** to our screen and only that! That's the equivalent of having a JavaScript function that looks like this:

```
function getDistance() {
  alert("42km");
}
```

Except for one very particular case, that JavaScript function doesn't seem very useful, does it? The way to increase the usefulness of this function is by modifying it to take arguments:

```
function getDistance(speed, time) {
    var result = speed * time;
    alert(result);
}
```

Now, your function can be used more generally for a variety of situations—not just one where the output will be **42km**.

Something similar applies to your components as well. Just like with functions, you can pass in arguments that alter what your component does. There is a slight terminology update you need to be on top of. What we call **arguments** in the function world are going to be known as **properties** in the component world. Let's see these properties in action!

We are going to modify our `HelloWorld` component to enable you to specify who or what you greet besides the generic **World**. For example, imagine being able to specify **Bono** as part of the `HelloWorld` call and seeing **Hello, Bono!** appear on screen.

To add properties to a component, there are two parts you need to follow.

First Part: Updating the Component Definition

Right now, our `HelloWorld` component is hard coded to always send out **Hello, world!** as part of its `return` value. The first thing we are going to do is change that behavior by having `return` print out the value passed in by a property. We need a name to give our property, and for this example, we are going to call our property **greetTarget**.

To specify the value of `greetTarget` as part of our component, here is the modification we need to make:

```
var HelloWorld = React.createClass({
  render: function() {
    return (
      <p>Hello, {this.props.greetTarget}!</p>
    );
  }
});
```

The way you access a property is by calling it via the `props` property that every component has access to. Notice how we specify this property. We place it inside curly brackets {and }. *In JSX, if you want something to get evaluated as an expression, you need to wrap that something inside curly brackets.* If you don't do that, you'll see the raw text `this.props.greetTarget` printed out.

Second Part: Modifying the Component Call

Once you've updated the component definition, all that remains is to pass in the property value as part of the component call. That is done by adding an attribute with the same name as our property, followed by the value you want to pass in. In our example, that would involve modifying the `HelloWorld` call with the `greetTarget` attribute and the value we want to give it.

Go ahead and modify our `HelloWorld` calls as follows:

```
ReactDOM.render(
  <div>
    <HelloWorld greetTarget="Batman"/>
    <HelloWorld greetTarget="Iron Man"/>
    <HelloWorld greetTarget="Nicolas Cage"/>
    <HelloWorld greetTarget="Mega Man"/>
    <HelloWorld greetTarget="Bono"/>
    <HelloWorld greetTarget="Catwoman"/>
  </div>,
  document.querySelector("#container")
);
```

Each of our `HelloWorld` calls now has the `greetTarget` attribute along with the name of a superhero (or equivalent mythical being!) that we wish to greet. If you preview this example in the browser, you'll see the greetings happily printed out on screen.

One last thing to call out before we move on. You are not limited to just having a single property on a component. You can have as many properties as you want, and your `props` property will easily accommodate any property requests you have without making any fuss.

Dealing with Children

A few sections ago, I mentioned that our components (in JSX) are very similar to regular HTML elements. We saw that for ourselves when we wrapped a component inside a `div` element or specified an attribute and value as part of specifying properties. There is one more thing you can do with components just like you can with many HTML elements. *Your components can have children.*

What this means is that you can do something like this:

```
<CleverComponent foo="bar">
  <p>Something!</p>
</CleverComponent>
```

You have a component very cleverly called `CleverComponent`, and it has a `p` element as a child. From within `CleverComponent`, you have the capability to access the `p` child element (and any children it may have) via the `children` property accessed by `this.props.children`.

To make sense of all this, let's fiddle with another really simple example. This time around, we have a component called `Buttonify` that wraps its children inside a button. The component looks like this:

```
var Buttonify = React.createClass({
  render: function() {
    return (
      <div>
        <button type={this.props.behavior}>{this.props.children}</button>
      </div>
    );
  }
});
```

The way you can use this component is by just calling it via the `ReactDOM.render` method as shown here:

```
ReactDOM.render(
  <div>
    <Buttonify behavior="Submit">SEND DATA</Buttonify>
  </div>,
  document.querySelector("#container")
);
```

When this code runs, given what the JSX in the `Buttonify` component's render method looked like, what you will see are the words "**SEND DATA**" wrapped inside a button element. With the appropriate styling, the result could look comically large like in Figure 3-4.

Figure 3-4   A large send data button.

Anyway, getting back to the JSX, notice that we specify a custom property called `behavior`. This property enables us to specify the `button` element's `type` attribute, and you can see us accessing it via `this.props.behavior` in the component definition's `render` method.

There is more to accessing a component's children than what we've seen here. For example, if your child element is the root of a deeply nested structure, the `this.props.children` property will return an array. If your child element is just a single element (like in our example), the `this.props.children` property returns a single component NOT wrapped inside an array. There are a few more things to call out, but instead of enumerating all the various cases and boring you, we'll naturally touch upon those cases as part of looking at more elaborate examples later on.

Conclusion

If you want to build an app using React, you can't wander too far without having to use a component. Trying to build a React app without using a component is kinda like building a JavaScript-based app without using functions. I am not saying that it can't be done. It is just one of those things you don't do...kinda like the *Bad Idea* part of the popular *Animaniacs Good Idea / Bad Idea* sketches you can find here: https://www.youtube.com/watch?v=2dJOIf4mdus:

If this witty video doesn't convince you why you should learn to embrace components, I don't know what will...except for maybe a future chapter on creating complex components! :P

4

Styling in React

For generations, mankind (and probably really smart dolphins) have styled their HTML content using CSS (aka Cascading Style Sheets). Things were good. With CSS, you had a good separation between the content and the presentation. The selector syntax gave you a lot of flexibility in choosing which elements to style and which ones to skip. You couldn't even find too many issues to hate about the *whole cascading thing* that CSS is all about.

Well, don't tell React that. While React doesn't actively hate CSS, it has a different view when it comes to styling content. As we've seen so far, one of React's core ideas is to have our app's visual pieces be self-contained and reusable. That is why the HTML elements and the JavaScript that impacts them are in the same bucket we call a component. We got a taste of that in the previous chapter.

What about how the HTML elements look (aka their styling)? Where should that go? You can probably guess where I am going with this. You can't have a self-contained piece of UI when the styling for it is defined somewhere else. That's why React encourages you to specify how your elements look right along side the HTML and the JavaScript. In this tutorial, you learn all about this mysterious (and possibly scandalous!) approach to styling your content. Of course, we also look at how to use CSS as well. There is room for both approaches—even if React may sorta kinda not think so :P

Onwards!

Displaying Some Vowels

To learn how to style our React content, let's work together on a (totally sweet and exciting!) example that simply displays vowels on a page. First, you'll need a blank HTML page that will host our React content. If you don't have one, feel free to use the following markup:

```
<!DOCTYPE html>
<html>

<head>
  <title>Styling in React</title>
  <script src="https://unpkg.com/react@15.3.2/dist/react.js"></script>
```

```html
<script src="https://unpkg.com/react-dom@15.3.2/dist/react-dom.js"></script>
<script src="https://cdnjs.cloudflare.com/ajax/libs/babel-core/5.8.23/browser.min
.js"></script>

<style>
  #container {
    padding: 50px;
    background-color: #FFF;
  }
</style>
</head>

<body>
  <div id="container"></div>

</body>

</html>
```

All this markup does is load in our React and Babel libraries and specify a div with an id value of **container**. To display the vowels, we're going to add some React-specific code.

Just below the **container** div element, add the following:

```html
<script type="text/babel">

  var Letter = React.createClass({
    render: function() {
        return (
          <div>
            {this.props.children}
          </div>
        );
      }
  });

  var destination = document.querySelector("#container");

  ReactDOM.render(
    <div>
      <Letter>A</Letter>
      <Letter>E</Letter>
      <Letter>I</Letter>
      <Letter>O</Letter>
      <Letter>U</Letter>
    </div>,
    destination
  );

</script>
```

From what we learned about components, nothing here should be a mystery. We create a component called `Letter` that is responsible for wrapping our vowels inside a `div` element. All of this is anchored in our HTML via a `script` tag whose type designates it as something Babel will know what to do with.

If you preview your page, you'll see something boring that looks like Figure 4-1.

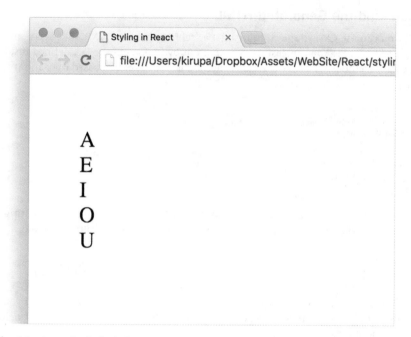

Figure 4-1   A boring output of what you see.

Don't worry, we'll make it look a little less boring in a few moments. After we've had a run at these letters, you will see something that looks more like Figure 4-2.

Figure 4-2   The letters arranged horizontally and with a yellow background.

Our vowels will be wrapped in a yellow background, aligned horizontally, and sport a fancy monospace font. Let's look at how to do all of this in both CSS as well as React's new-fangled approach.

Styling React Content Using CSS

Using CSS to style our React content is actually as straightforward as you can imagine it to be. Because React ends up spitting out regular HTML tags, all of the various CSS tricks you've learned over the years to style HTML still apply. There are just a few minor things to keep in mind.

Understand the Generated HTML

Before you can use CSS, you need to first get a feel for what the HTML that React spits out is going to look like. You can easily figure that out by looking at the JSX defined inside the `render` methods. The parent `render` method is our `ReactDOM` based one, and it looks as follows:

```
<div>
    <Letter>A</Letter>
    <Letter>E</Letter>
    <Letter>I</Letter>
    <Letter>O</Letter>
    <Letter>U</Letter>
</div>
```

We have our various `Letter` components wrapped inside a `div`. Nothing too exciting here. The `render` method inside our `Letter` component isn't that much different either:

```
<div>
    {this.props.children}
</div>
```

As you can see, each individual vowel is wrapped inside its own set of `div` tags. If you had to play this all out (such as, previewing our example in a browser), the final DOM structure for our vowels looks like Figure 4-3.

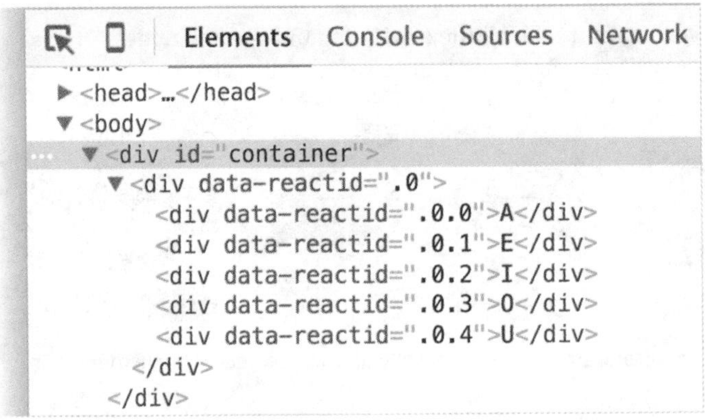

Figure 4-3   The preview from inside the browser.

Ignore the `data-reacroot` attribute (that you may not even see depending on your version of React!) on the **container** `div`, but pay attention to the rest of the things you see. What we have is simply an HTML-ized expansion of the various JSX fragments we saw in the `render` method a few moments ago with our vowels nested inside a bunch of `div` elements.

Just Style It Already!

Once you understand the HTML arrangement of the things you want to style, the hard part is done. Now comes the fun and familiar part of defining style selectors and specifying the properties you want to set. To affect our inner `div` elements, add the following inside our `style` tag:

```
div div div {
  padding: 10px;
  margin: 10px;
  background-color: #ffde00;
  color: #333;
  display: inline-block;
  font-family: monospace;
  font-size: 32px;
  text-align: center;
}
```

The `div div div` selector will ensure we style the right things. The end result will be our vowels styled to look exactly like we saw earlier. With that said, a style selector of `div div div` looks a bit odd, doesn't it? It is too generic. In apps with more than three nested `div` elements (which will be very common), you may end up styling the wrong things. It is at times like this where you will want to change the HTML that React generates to make our content more easily style-able.

The way we are going to address this is by giving our inner `div` elements a `class` value of **letter**. Here is where JSX differs from HTML. Make the following highlighted change:

```
var Letter = React.createClass({
  render: function() {
      return (
        <div className="letter">
          {this.props.children}
        </div>
      );
    }
});
```

Notice that we designate the class value by using the `className` attribute instead of the `class` attribute. The reason has to do with the word *class* being a special keyword in JavaScript. If that doesn't make any sense why it is important, don't worry about it for now. We'll cover that later.

Anyway, once you've given your div a className attribute value of **letter**, there is just one more thing to do. Modify the CSS selector to target our div elements more cleanly:

```css
.letter {
  padding: 10px;
  margin: 10px;
  background-color: #ffde00;
  color: #333;
  display: inline-block;
  font-family: monospace;
  font-size: 32px;
  text-align: center;
}
```

As you can see, using CSS is a perfectly viable way to style the content in your React-based apps. In the next section, we'll look at how to style our content using the approach preferred by React.

Styling Content the React Way

React favors an inline approach for styling content that doesn't use CSS. While that seems a bit strange at first, it is designed to help make your visuals more reusable. The goal is to have your components be little black boxes where everything related to how your UI looks and works gets stashed there. Let's see this for ourselves.

Continuing our example from earlier, remove the .letter style rule. Once you have done this, your vowels will return to their unstyled state when you preview your app in the browser. For completeness, you should remove the className declaration from our Letter component's render function as well. There is no point having our markup contain things we won't be using.

Right now, our Letter component is back to its original state:

```javascript
var Letter = React.createClass({
  render: function() {
      return (
        <div>
          {this.props.children}
        </div>
      );
    }
});
```

The way you specify styles inside your component is by defining an object whose content is the CSS properties and their values. Once you have that object, you assign that object to the JSX elements you wish to style by using the style attribute. This will make more sense once we perform these two steps ourselves, so let's apply all of this to style the output of our Letter component.

Creating a Style Object

Let's get right to it by defining our object that contains the styles we wish to apply:

```
var Letter = React.createClass({
  render: function() {
    var letterStyle = {
      padding: 10,
      margin: 10,
      backgroundColor: "#ffde00",
      color: "#333",
      display: "inline-block",
      fontFamily: "monospace",
      fontSize: 32,
      textAlign: "center"
    };

    return (
      <div>
        {this.props.children}
      </div>
    );
  }
});
```

We have an object called `letterStyle`, and the properties inside it are just CSS property names and their value. If you've never defined CSS properties in JavaScript before (i.e., by setting `object.style`), the formula for converting them into something JavaScript-friendly is pretty simple:

- Single word CSS properties (like `padding`, `margin`, `color`) remain unchanged.

- Multi-word CSS properties with a dash in them (like `background-color`, `font-family`, `border-radius`) are turned into one camelcase word with the dash removed and the words following the dash capitalized. For example, using our example properties, `background-color` would become `backgroundColor`, font-family would become `fontFamily`, and `border-radius` would become `borderRadius`.

Our `letterStyle` object and its properties are pretty much a direct JavaScript translation of the `.letter` style rule we looked at a few moments ago. All that remains now is to assign this object to the element we wish to style.

Actually Styling Our Content

Now that we have our object containing the styles we wish to apply, the rest is very easy. Find the element we wish to apply the style to and set the `style` attribute to refer to that object. In our case, that will be the `div` element returned by our `Letter` component's `render` function.

Take a look at the highlighted line to see how this is done for our example:

```
var Letter = React.createClass({
  render: function() {
      var letterStyle = {
        padding: 10,
        margin: 10,
        backgroundColor: "#ffde00",
        color: "#333",
        display: "inline-block",
        fontFamily: "monospace",
        fontSize: "32",
        textAlign: "center"
      };

      return (
        <div style={letterStyle}>
          {this.props.children}
        </div>
      );
    }
});
```

Our object is called letterStyle, so that is what we specify inside the curly brackets to let React know to evaluate the expression. That's all there is to it. Go ahead and run the example in the browser to ensure everything works properly and all of our vowels are properly styled.

For some extra validation, if you inspect the styling applied to one of the vowels using your browser developer tool of choice, you'll see that the styles are infact applied inline (see Figure 4-4).

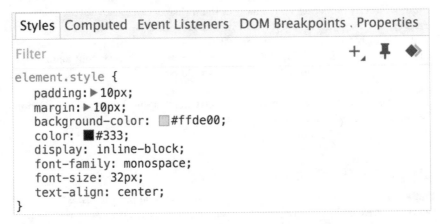

Figure 4-4 The styles are applied inline.

While this is no surprise, it might be difficult for those of us used to styles being inside style rules to swallow. As they say, the Times They Are A Changin' (https://www.youtube.com/watch?v=e7qQ6_RV4VQ).

You Can Omit the "px" Suffix

When programmatically setting styles, it's a pain to deal with numbers that need a pixel value suffix. In order to generate these values, you need to do some string concatenation on your number to add a *px*. To convert from a pixel value back to a number, you need to parse out the *px*. All of this isn't extremely complicated or time consuming, but it is a distraction.

To help with this, React allows you to omit the *px* suffix for a bunch of CSS properties. If you recall, our `letterStyle` object looks as follows:

```
 1   var letterStyle = {
 2     padding: 10,
 3     margin: 10,
 4     backgroundColor: "#ffde00",
 5     color: "#333",
 6     display: "inline-block",
 7     fontFamily: "monospace",
 8     fontSize: "32",
 9     textAlign: "center"
10   };=
```

Notice that for some of the properties with a numerical value such as `padding`, `margin`, and `fontSize`, we didn't specify the *px* suffix at all. That is because, at runtime, React will add the *px* suffix automatically.

The only number-related properties React won't add a pixel suffix to automatically are the following properties: `animationIterationCount`, `boxFlex`, `boxFlexGroup`, `boxOrdinal-Group`, `columnCount`, `fillOpacity`, `flex`, `flexGrow`, `flexPositive`, `flexShrink`, `flex-Negative`, `flexOrder`, `fontWeight`, `lineClamp`, `lineHeight`, `opacity`, `order`, `orphans`, `stopOpacity`, `strokeDashoffset`, `strokeOpacity`, `strokeWidth`, `tabSize`, `widows`, `zIndex`, and `zoom`. While I wish I could tell you that I walk around with this information memorized, I actually just referred to this article: https://facebook.github.io/react/tips/style-props-value-px .html Please hold your applause :P

While pixel values are great for many things, you may want to use percentages, ems, vh, etc. to represent your values. For these non-pixel values, you still have to manually ensure the suffix is dealt with. React won't help you out there, so if you aren't a fan of pixel values, this nicety doesn't gain you much.

Making the Background Color Customizable

The last thing we are going to do before we wrap things up is take advantage of how React works with styles. By having our styles defined in the same vicinity as the JSX, we can make the various style values easily customizable by the parent (aka the consumer of the component). Let's see this in action.

Right now, all of our vowels have a yellow background. Wouldn't it be cool if we could specify the background color as part of each `Letter` declaration? To do this, in our `ReactDOM.render` method, first add a `bgcolor` attribute and specify some colors as shown in the following highlighted lines:

```
ReactDOM.render(
  <div>
    <Letter bgcolor="#58B3FF">A</Letter>
    <Letter bgcolor="#FF605F">E</Letter>
    <Letter bgcolor="#FFD52E">I</Letter>
    <Letter bgcolor="#49DD8E">O</Letter>
    <Letter bgcolor="#AE99FF">U</Letter>
  </div>,
  destination
);
```

Next, we need to use this property. In our `letterStyle` object, set the value of `background-Color` to `this.props.bgColor`:

```
1   var letterStyle = {
2       padding: 10,
3       margin: 10,
4       backgroundColor: this.props.bgcolor,
5       color: "#333",
6       display: "inline-block",
7       fontFamily: "monospace",
8       fontSize: "32",
9       textAlign: "center"
10  };
```

This will ensure that the `backgroundColor` value is inferred from what we set via the `bgColor` attribute as part of the `Letter` declaration. If you preview this in your browser, you will now see our same vowels sporting some totally sweet background colors as shown in Figure 4-5.

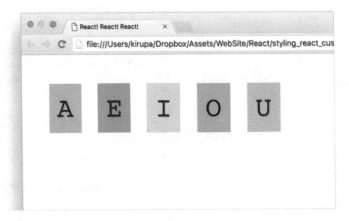

Figure 4-5   Our vowels with background colors!

What we've just done is something that is going to be very hard to replicate using plain CSS. Now, as we start to look at components whose contents change based on state or user interaction, you'll see more such examples where the React way of styling things has a lot of good merit.

Conclusion

As we dive in further and learn more about React, you'll see several more cases where React does things quite differently than what we've been told is the correct way of doing things on the web. In this tutorial, we saw React promoting inline styles in JavaScript as a way to style content as opposed to using CSS style rules. Earlier, we looked at JSX and how the entirety of your UI can be declared in JavaScript using an XML-like syntax that sorta kinda looks like HTML.

In all of these cases, if you look deeper beneath the surface, the reasons for why React diverges from conventional wisdom makes a lot of sense. Building apps with their very complex UI requirements requires a new way of solving the challenges associated with complex UIs. HTML, CSS, and JavaScript techniques that probably made a lot of sense when dealing with web pages and documents may not be applicable in the web app world where components are re-used inside other components.

With that said, you should pick and choose the techniques that make the most sense for your situation. While I am biased towards React's way of solving our UI development problems, I'll do my best to highlight alternate or conventional methods as well. Tying that back to what we saw here, using CSS style rules with your React content is totally OK as long as you make the decision knowing the things you gain as well as lose by doing so.

5

Creating Complex Components

In Chapter 3, you learned about components and all the awesome things that they do. You learned that components are the primary ways through which React enables our visual elements to behave like little reusable bricks that contain all of the HTML, JavaScript, and styling needed to run themselves. Beyond reusability, there is another major advantage components bring to the table. They make possible **composability**. You can combine components to create more complex components.

In this chapter, we look at what all of this means. More specifically, we look at two things:

- The boring technical stuff that you need to know.
- The boring stuff you need to know about how to identify components when you look at a bunch of visual elements.

OK, what you are going to learn isn't actually *that* boring. I am just setting your expectations really low :P

From Visuals to Components

The various examples we've looked at so far have been pretty basic. They were great for highlighting technical concepts (see Figure 5-1), but they weren't great for preparing you for the real world.

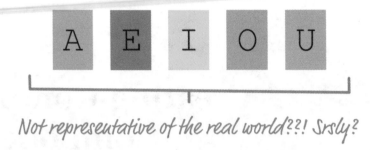

Not representative of the real world??! Srsly?

Figure 5-1   Great for highlighting technical concepts, but...

In the real world, what you'll be asked to implement in React will never be so simple as a list of names or colorful blocks of vowels. Instead, you'll be given a visual representation of some complex user interface. That visual can take many forms—a scribble, diagram, screenshot, video, redline, comp, etc. It is up to you to bring all of those static pixels to life, and we are going to get some hands-on practice in doing just that.

What we are going to do is build a simple color palette card (see Figure 5-2).

#FF6663

Hi! I am a simple color palette card :P

Figure 5-2   A simple color palette card.

If you are not sure what these are, these are small rectangular cards that help you match a color with a particular type of paint. You'll frequently see them in home improvement stores or anywhere paint is sold. Your designer friend probably has a giant closet dedicated to them in their place. Anyway, *our mission is to recreate one of these cards using React.*

There are several ways to go about this, but I am going to show you a very systematic approach that will help you simplify and make sense of even the most complex user interfaces. This approach involves two steps:

1. Identify the major visual elements

2. Figure out what the components will be

Both of these steps sound really complex, but as we walk through this, you'll see that it is nothing to be worried about.

Identifying the Major Visual Elements

The first step is to identify all of the visual elements we are dealing with. No visual element is too minor to omit—at least not initially. The easiest way to start identifying the relevant pieces is to start with the obvious visual elements and then dive into the less obvious ones.

The first thing you will see in our example is the card itself (see Figure 5.3).

Figure 5-3   The card.

Within the card, you'll see that there are two distinct regions. The top region is a rectangular area that displays a particular color. The bottom region is a white area that displays a hex value.

Let's call out these two visual elements and arrange them into a tree-like structure as shown in Figure 5-4.

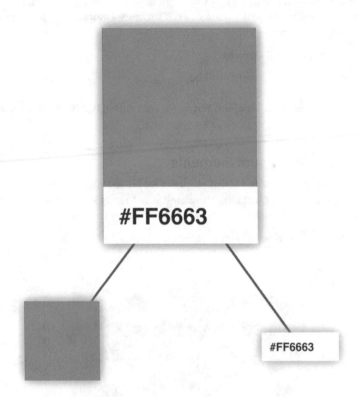

Figure 5-4   Tree-like structure.

Arranging your visuals into this tree-like structure (aka a **visual hierarchy**) is a good way to get a better feel for how your visual elements are grouped. The goal of this exercise is to identify the important visual elements and break them into a parent/child arrangement until you can divide them no further.

Try to Ignore Implementation Details

While it is hard, do not think of implementation details yet. Don't focus on dividing your visual elements based on what combination of HTML and CSS would be required. There is plenty of time for that later!

Continuing on, we can see that our colorful rectangle isn't something that we can divide further. That doesn't mean we are done, though. We can further divide the label from the white region that surrounds it. Right now, our visual hierarchy looks as shown in Figure 5-5 with our label and white region occupying a separate spot in our tree.

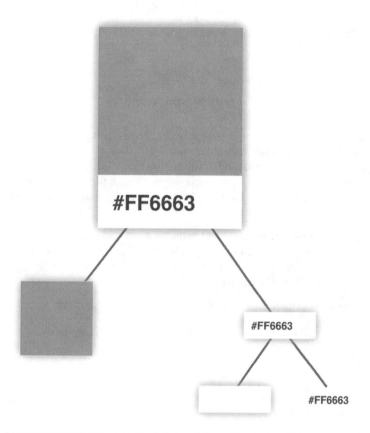

Figure 5-5 Dividing things further into the label and the white region that surrounds it.

At this point, we have nothing else to divide any further. We are done with identifying and dividing up our visual elements, so the next step is to use what we've found here to help us identify the components.

Identifying the Components

This is where things get a little interesting. We need to figure out which of the visual elements we've identified will be turned into a component and which ones will not. Not every visual element will need to be turned into a component, and we certainly don't want to create only a few extremely complex components either. There needs to be a balance (see Figure 5-6).

too few   *TOO MANY!!!*

Figure 5-6   Not too few and not too many components.

There is an art to figuring out what visual elements become part of a component and which ones don't. *The general rule is that our components should do just one thing*. If you find that your potential component will end up doing too many things, you probably want to break your component into multiple components. On the flip side, if your potential component does too little, you probably want to skip making that visual element a component altogether.

Let's try to figure out which elements would make for good components in our example. From looking at our visual hierarchy, right off the bat, both the card and the colored rectangle seem like they fit the bill for making a great component. The card acts as the outer container, and the colored rectangle simply displays a color.

That just puts a question mark around our label and the white region it is surrounded by though (see Figure 5-7).

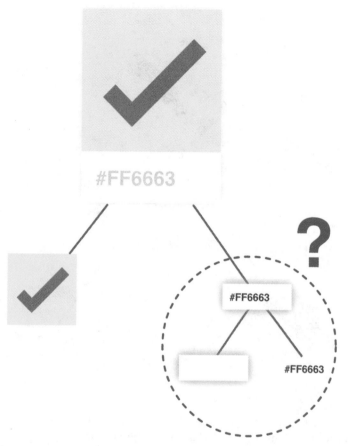

Figure 5-7   Question mark around the label and the white space around it.

The important part here is the label itself. Without it, we can't see the hex value. That leaves just the white region. The purpose it serves is negligible. It is simply empty space, and the responsibility for that can easily be handed off to our label itself. Brace yourself for what I am about to say next. Sadly, our white rectangular region will not be turned into a component.

At this point, we have identified our three components, and the **component hierarchy** looks as in Figure 5-8.

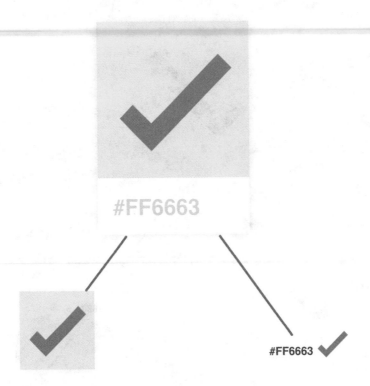

Figure 5-8   The three components.

An important thing to note is that the component hierarchy has more to do with helping us define our code than it does with how the finished product will look. You'll notice that it looks a bit different than the visual hierarchy we started off with. For visual details, you should always refer to your source material (aka your visual comps, redlines, screenshots, and other related items). For figuring out which components to create, you should use the component hierarchy.

Ok, now that we've identified our components and the relationship between all of them, it is time to start bringing our color palette card to life.

Creating the Components

This is the easy part—sort of! It is time for us to start writing some code. The first thing we need is a mostly-empty HTML page that will serve as our starting point:

```
<!DOCTYPE html>
<html>

<head>
  <title>More Components!</title>
```

```
  <script src="https://unpkg.com/react@15.3.2/dist/react.js"></script>
  <script src="https://unpkg.com/react-dom@15.3.2/dist/react-dom.js"></script>
  <script src="https://cdnjs.cloudflare.com/ajax/libs/babel-core/5.8.23/browser.min
.js"></script>

  <style>
    #container {
      padding: 50px;
      background-color: #FFF;
    }
  </style>
</head>

<body>
  <div id="container"></div>
  <script type="text/babel">

    ReactDOM.render(
      <div>

      </div>,
      document.querySelector("#container")
    );
  </script>
</body>

</html>
```

Take a moment to see what this page has going on. There isn't much—just the bare minimum needed to have React render an empty `div` into our **container** element.

After you've done this, it is time to define our three components. The names we will go with for our components will be **Card**, **Label**, and **Square**. Go ahead and add the following highlighted lines just above the `ReactDOM.render` function:

```
var Square = React.createClass({
  render: function() {
    return(
      <p>Nothing</p>
    );
  }
});

var Label = React.createClass({
  render: function() {
    return (
      <p>Nothing</p>
    );
```

```
    }
});

var Card = React.createClass({
  render: function() {
      return (

      );
    }
});
```

```
ReactDOM.render(
  <div>

  </div>,
  document.querySelector("#container")
);
```

Within our three components, we also threw in the render function that each component absolutely needs to function. Other than that, our components are empty. In the following sections, we will fix that by filling them in.

The Card Component

We are going to start at the top of our component hierarchy and focus on our Card component first. This component will act as the the container that our Square and Label components will live in.

To implement it, go ahead and make the following highlighted modifications:

```
 1 | var Card = React.createClass({
 2 |   render: function() {
 3 |       var cardStyle = {
 4 |         height: 200,
 5 |         width: 150,
 6 |         padding: 0,
 7 |         backgroundColor: "#FFF",
 8 |         WebkitFilter: "drop-shadow(0px 0px 5px #666)",
 9 |         filter: "drop-shadow(0px 0px 5px #666)"
10 |       };
11 |
12 |       return (
13 |         <div style={cardStyle}>
14 |
15 |         </div>
16 |       );
17 |     }
18 | });
```

While this seems like a lot of changes, the bulk of the lines are going into styling the output of our Card component via the cardStyle object. Inside the object, notice that we specify a vendor-prefixed version of the CSS filter property with WebkitFilter. That's not the interesting detail. The interesting detail is the capitalization. Instead of the first letter being camel-cased as *webkitFilter*, the W is actually capitalized. That isn't how other normal CSS properties are represented, so keep that in mind if you ever need to specify a vendor-prefixed property.

The rest of the changes are pretty unimpressive. We return a div element, and that element's style attribute is set to our cardStyle object. Now, to see our Card component in action, we need to display it in our DOM as part of the ReactDOM.render function. To make that happen, go ahead and make the following highlighted change:

```
1 | ReactDOM.render(
2 |   <div>
3 |     <Card/>
4 |   </div>,
5 |   document.querySelector("#container")
6 | );
```

All we are doing is telling the ReactDOM.render function to render the output of our Card component by invoking it. If everything worked out properly, you'll see the same thing as in Figure 5-9 if you test your app.

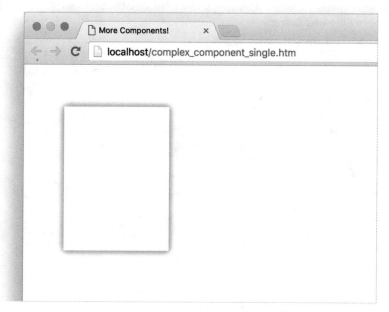

Figure 5-9   The result of your test—the outline of the color palette card.

Yes, it is just the outline of our color palette card, but that is definitely more than what we started out with just a few moments ago!

The Square Component

It's time to go one level down in our component hierarchy and look at our `Square` component. This is a pretty straightforward one, so make the following highlighted changes:

```
 1  var Square = React.createClass({
 2    render: function() {
 3      var squareStyle = {
 4        height: 150,
 5        backgroundColor: "#FF6663"
 6      };
 7      return(
 8        <div style={squareStyle}>
 9
10        </div>
11      );
12    }
13  });
```

Just like with our `Card` component, we are returning a `div` element whose `style` attribute is set to a `style` object that defines how this component looks. To see our `Square` component in action, we need to get it onto our DOM just like we did with the `Card` component earlier. The difference this time around is that we won't be calling the `Square` component via our `ReactDOM.render` function. Instead, we'll call the `Square` component from inside the `Card` component. To see what I mean, go back to our `Card` component's render function, and make the following change:

```
var Card = React.createClass({
  render: function() {
    var cardStyle = {
      height: 200,
      width: 150,
      padding: 0,
      backgroundColor: "#FFF",
      WebkitFilter: "drop-shadow(0px 0px 5px #666)",
      filter: "drop-shadow(0px 0px 5px #666)"
    };

    return (
      <div style={cardStyle}>
        <Square/>
      </div>
    );
  }
});
```

At this point, if you preview our app, you'll see a colorful square making an appearance (see Figure 5-10).

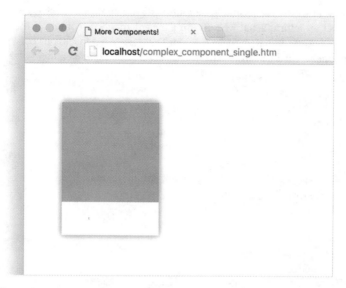

Figure 5-10   The red portion appears.

The cool thing to call out is that we called our Square component from inside the Card component! This is an example of **component composability** where one component relies on the output of another component. The final thing you see is the result of these two components colluding with each other. Isn't collusion just beautiful—at least in this context?

The Label Component

The last component that remains is our Label. Go ahead and make the following highlighted changes:

```
 1 | var Label = React.createClass({
 2 |   render: function() {
 3 |     var labelStyle = {
 4 |       fontFamily: "sans-serif",
 5 |       fontWeight: "bold",
 6 |       padding: 13,
 7 |       margin: 0
 8 |     };
 9 |
10 |     return (
11 |       <p style={labelStyle}>#FF6663</p>
12 |     );
13 |   }
14 | });
```

The pattern of what we are doing should be routine to you by now. We have a `style` object that we assign to what we return. What we return is a p element whose content is the string #FF6663. To have what we return ultimately make it to our DOM, we need to call our `Label` component via our `Card` component. Go ahead and make the following highlighted change:

```
 1 | var Card = React.createClass({
 2 |   render: function() {
 3 |     var cardStyle = {
 4 |       height: 200,
 5 |       width: 150,
 6 |       padding: 0,
 7 |       backgroundColor: "#FFF",
 8 |       WebkitFilter: "drop-shadow(0px 0px 5px #666)",
 9 |       filter: "drop-shadow(0px 0px 5px #666)"
10 |     };
11 |
12 |     return (
13 |       <div style={cardStyle}>
14 |         <Square/>
15 |         <Label/>
16 |       </div>
17 |     );
18 |   }
19 | });
```

Notice that our `Label` component lives just under the `Square` component we added to our `Card` component's return function earlier. If you preview your app in the browser now, you should see something that looks like Figure 5-11.

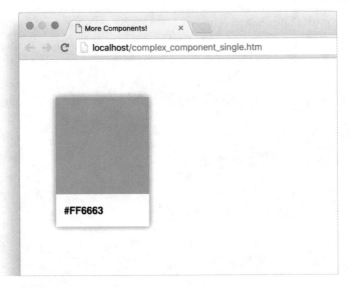

Figure 5-11   The label appears.

Yes, that's right! Our color palette card is done and visible, thanks to the efforts of our `Card`, `Square`, and `Label` components. That doesn't mean we are done yet, though. There are a few more things to cover.

Passing Properties, Again!

In our current example, we hard-coded the color value that is used by our `Square` and `Label` components. That is an odd thing to do—which may or may not have been done deliberately for dramatic effect, but fixing it is straightforward. It just involves us specifying a property name and accessing it via `this.props`. We've seen all this before. What is different is the number of times we will have to do this.

There is no way to *properly* specify a property on a parent component and have all descendants automatically gain access to that property. There are many *improper* ways to deal with this such as defining global objects, setting the value on a component property directly, and so on. We won't concern ourselves with such improper solutions right now. We aren't animals!

Anyway, the proper way to pass a property value to a child component is to have each intermediate parent component pass on the property as well. To see this in action, take a look at the highlighted changes to our current code where we move away from a hard-coded color and define our card's color using a `color` property instead:

```
 1 | var Square = React.createClass({
 2 |   render: function() {
 3 |     var squareStyle = {
 4 |       height: 150,
 5 |       backgroundColor: this.props.color
 6 |     };
 7 |     return(
 8 |       <div style={squareStyle}>
 9 |
10 |       </div>
11 |     );
12 |   }
13 | });
14 |
15 | var Label = React.createClass({
16 |   render: function() {
17 |     var labelStyle = {
18 |       fontFamily: "sans-serif",
19 |       fontWeight: "bold",
20 |       padding: 13,
21 |       margin: 0
22 |     };
23 |
24 |     return (
25 |       <p style={labelStyle}>{this.props.color}</p>
```

```
26        );
27      }
28    });
29
30    var Card = React.createClass({
31      render: function() {
32          var cardStyle = {
33            height: 200,
34            width: 150,
35            padding: 0,
36            backgroundColor: "#FFF",
37            WebkitFilter: "drop-shadow(0px 0px 5px #666)",
38            filter: "drop-shadow(0px 0px 5px #666)"
39          };
40
41          return (
42            <div style={cardStyle}>
43              <Square color={this.props.color}/>
44              <Label color={this.props.color}/>
45            </div>
46          );
47      }
48    });
49
50    ReactDOM.render(
51      <div>
52        <Card color="#FF6663"/>
53      </div>,
54      document.querySelector("#container")
55    );
```

Once you have made this change, you can specify any hex color you want as part of calling the Card component:

```
1    ReactDOM.render(
2      <div>
3        <Card color="#FFA737"/>
4      </div>,
5      document.querySelector("#container")
6    );
```

The resulting color palette card will feature the color you specified (see Figure 5-12).

#FFA737

Figure 5-12   The color for hex value #FFA737.

Now, let's go back to the changes we made. Even though the `color` property is only consumed by the `Square` and `Label` components, the parent `Card` component is responsible for passing the property on to them. For even more deeply nested situations, you'll have more intermediate components that will be responsible for transferring properties. It gets worse. When you have multiple properties that you would like to pass around multiple levels of components, the amount of typing (or copying/pasting) you do increases a lot as well. There are ways to mitigate this, and we'll look at those mitigation strategies in much greater detail in a future chapter.

Why Component Composability Rocks

When we are heads-down in React, we often tend to forgot that what we are ultimately creating is just plain and boring HTML, CSS, and JavaScript. The generated HTML for our color palette card looks as follows:

```
<div id="container">
  <div data-reactid=".0">
    <div style="height:200px;
                width:150px;
                padding:0;
                background-color:#FFF;
                -webkit-filter:drop-shadow(0px 0px 5px #666);
                filter:drop-shadow(0px 0px 5px #666);">
      <div style="height:150px;
                  background-color:#FF6663;"></div>
      <p style="font-family:sans-serif;
                font-weight:bold;
                padding:13px;
                margin:0;">#FF6663</p>
    </div>
  </div>
</div>
```

This markup has no idea of how it got there. It doesn't know about which components were responsible for what. It doesn't care about component composability or the frustrating way we had to transfer the color property from parent to child. That brings up an important point to make.

If we had to generalize the end result of what components do, **all they do is return blobs of HTML to whatever called it**. Each component's render function returns some HTML to another component's render function. All of this HTML keeps accumulating until a giant blob of HTML is pushed (very efficiently) to our DOM. That simplicity is why component re-use and composability works so well. Each blob of HTML works independently from other blobs of HTML—especially if you specify inline styles as React recommends. This enables you to easily create visual elements from other visual elements without having to worry about anything. ANYTHING! Isn't that pretty freaking awesome?

Conclusion

As you may have realized by now, we are slowly shifting focus towards the more advanced scenarios that React thrives in. Actually, advanced isn't the right word. The correct word is *realistic*. In this chapter, we started by learning how to look at a piece of UI and identify the components in a way that you can later implement. That is a situation you will find yourself in all the time. While the approach we employed seemed really formal, as you get more experienced with creating things in React, you can ratchet down the formality. If you can quickly identify the components and their parent/child relationships without creating a visual and component hierarchy, then that is one more sign that you are getting really good at working with React!

Identifying the components is only one part of the equation. The other part is bringing those components to life. Most of the technical stuff we saw here was just a minor extension of what we've already seen earlier. We looked at one level of components in an earlier chapter, and here we looked at how to work with multiple levels of components. We looked at how to pass properties between one parent and one child in an earlier chapter, and here we looked at how to pass properties between multiple parents and multiple children. Maybe in a future chapter we'll do something groundbreaking like drawing multiple color palette cards to the screen! Or, we can maybe specify two properties instead of just a single one. Who knows?

6

Transferring Properties (Props)

There is a frustrating side to working with properties. We kinda saw this side in the previous chapter. Passing properties from one component to another is nice and simple when you are dealing with only one layer of components. When you wish to send a property across multiple layers of components, things start getting complicated.

Things getting complicated is never a good thing, so in this chapter, let's see what we can do to make working with properties across multiple layers of components easy.

Problem Overview

Let's say that you have a deeply nested component, and its hierarchy (modeled as awesomely colored circles) looks like Figure 6-1.

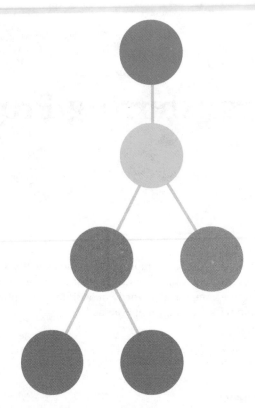

Figure 6-1   The component hierarchy.

What you want to do is pass a property from your red circle all the way down to our purple circles where it will be used. What we can't do is the very obvious and straightforward thing shown in Figure 6-2.

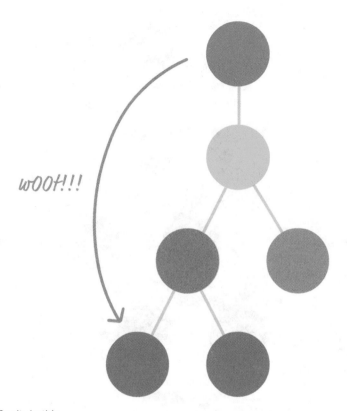

woot!!!

Figure 6-2   Can't do this.

You can't pass a property directly to the component or components that you wish to target. The reason has to do with how React works. *React enforces a chain of command where properties have to flow down from a parent component to an immediate child component.* This means you can't skip a layer of children when sending a property. This also means your children can't send a property back up to a parent. All communication is one-way from the parent to the child.

Under these guidelines, passing a property from our red circle to our purple circle looks a little bit like Figure 6-3.

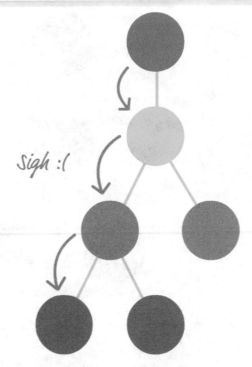

Figure 6-3   The property is passed from parent to child.

Every component that lies on the intended path has to receive the property from its parent and then re-send that property to its child. This process repeats until your property reaches its intended destination. The problem is in this receiving and re-sending step.

If we had to send a property called `color` from the component representing our red circle to the component representing our purple circle, its path to the destination would look something like Figure 6-4.

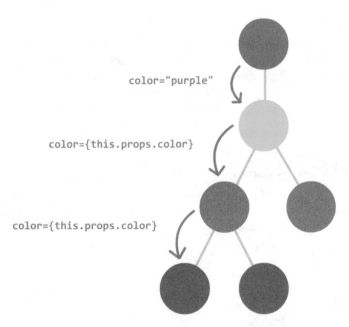

Figure 6-4   Sending the `color` property.

Now, imagine we have two properties that we need to send, as in Figure 6-5.

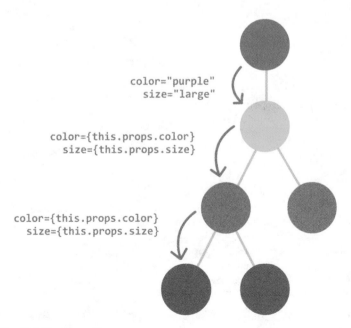

Figure 6-5   Sending two properties.

What if we wanted to send three properties? Or four?

We can quickly see that this approach is neither scalable nor maintainable. For every additional property we need to communicate, we are going to have to add an entry for it as part of declaring each component. If we decide to rename our properties at some point, we will have to ensure that every instance of that property is renamed as well. If we remove a property, we need to remove the property from every component that relied on it. Overall, these are the kinds of situations we try to avoid when writing code. What can we do about this?

Detailed Look at the Problem

In the previous section, we talked at a high level about what the problem is. Before we can dive into figuring out a solution, we need to go beyond diagrams and look at a more detailed example with real code. We need to take a look at something like the following:

```javascript
var Display = React.createClass({
  render: function() {
    return(
      <div>
        <p>{this.props.color}</p>
        <p>{this.props.num}</p>
        <p>{this.props.size}</p>
      </div>
    );
  }
});

var Label = React.createClass({
  render: function() {
    return (
      <Display color={this.props.color}
               num={this.props.num}
               size={this.props.size}/>
    );
  }
});

var Shirt = React.createClass({
  render: function() {
    return (
      <div>
        <Label color={this.props.color}
               num={this.props.num}
               size={this.props.size}/>
      </div>
    );
  }
});
```

```
ReactDOM.render(
  <div>
    <Shirt color="steelblue" num="3.14" size="medium"/>
  </div>,
  document.querySelector("#container")
);
```

Take a few moments to understand what is going on. Once you have done that, let's walk through this example together.

What we have is a `Shirt` component that relies on the output of the `Label` component which relies on the output of the `Display` component. (Try saying that sentence five time fast!) Anyway, the component hierarchy can be seen in Figure 6-6.

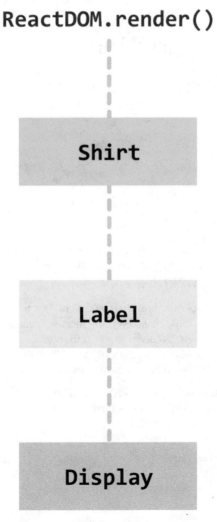

Figure 6-6   The component hierarchy.

When you run this code, what gets output is nothing special. It is just three lines of text (see Figure 6-7).

Figure 6-7   The three lines of text.

The interesting part is how the text gets there. Each of the three lines of text that you see maps to a property we specified at the very beginning inside ReactDOM.render:

```
<Shirt color="steelblue" num="3.14" size="medium"/>
```

The color, num, and size properties (and their values) make a journey all the way to the Display component that would make even the most seasoned world traveler jealous. Let's follow these properties from their inception to when they get consumed, and I do realize that a lot of this will be a review of what you've already seen. If you find yourself getting bored, feel free to skip on to the next section. With that said, onwards and upwards!

Life for our properties starts inside ReactDOM.render when our Shirt component gets called with the color, num, and size properties specified:

```
ReactDOM.render(
  <div>
    <Shirt color="steelblue" num="3.14" size="medium"/>
  </div>,
  document.querySelector("#container")
);
```

We not only define the properties, we also initialize them with the values they will carry.

Inside the `Shirt` component, these properties are stored inside the `props` object. To transfer these properties on, we need to explicitly access these properties from the `props` object and list them as part of the component call. The following is an example of what that looks like when our `Shirt` component calls our `Label` component:

```
var Shirt = React.createClass({
  render: function() {
      return (
        <div>
          <Label color={this.props.color}
                 num={this.props.num}
                 size={this.props.size}/>
        </div>
      );
    }
});
```

Notice that the `color`, `num`, and `size` properties are listed again. The only difference from what we saw with the `ReactDOM.render` call is that the values for each property are taken from their respective entry in the `props` object as opposed to being manually entered.

When our `Label` component goes live, it has its `props` object properly filled out with the `color`, `num`, and `size` properties stored. You can probably see a pattern forming here. If you need to let out a big yawn, feel free to.

The `Label` component continues the tradition by repeating the same steps and calling the `Display` component:

```
var Label = React.createClass({
  render: function() {
    return (
      <Display color={this.props.color}
               num={this.props.num}
               size={this.props.size}/>
    );
  }
});
```

Phew. All we wanted to do was have our `Display` component display some values for `color`, `num`, and `size`. The only complication was that the values we wanted to display were originally defined as part of `ReactDOM.render`. The annoying solution is the one you see here where every component along the path to the destination needs to access and re-define each property as part of passing it along. That's just terrible. We can do better than this, and you will see how in a few moments!

Meet the Spread Operator

The solution to all of our problems lies in something new to JavaScript known as the **spread operator**. What the spread operator does is a bit bizarre to explain without some context, so I'll first give you an example and then bore you with a definition.

Take a look at the following snippet:

```
var items = ["1", "2", "3"];

function printStuff(a, b, c) {
  console.log("Printing: " + a + " " + b + " " + c);
}
```

We have an array called `items` that contains three values. We also have a function called `printStuff` that takes three arguments. What we want to do is specify the three values from our `items` array as arguments to the `printStuff` function. Sounds simple enough, right?

Here is one really common way of doing that:

```
printStuff(items[0], items[1], items[2]);
```

We access each array item individually and pass it in to our `printStuff` function. With the spread operator, we now have an easier way. You don't have to specify each item in the array individually at all. You can just do something like this:

```
printStuff(...items);
```

The spread operator is the ... characters before our `items` array, and using ...`items` is identical to listing `items[0]`, `items[1]`, and `items[2]` individually like we did earlier. The `printStuff` function will run and print the numbers 1, 2, and 3 to our console. Pretty cool, right?

Now that you've seen the spread operator in action, it's time to define it. *The spread operator enables you to unwrap an array into its individual elements.* The spread operator does a few more things as well, but that's not important for now. We are going to only use this particular side of the spread operator to solve our property transferring problem!

Properly Transferring Properties

We just saw an example where we used the spread operator to avoid having to enumerate every single item in our array as part of passing it to a function:

```
var items = ["1", "2", "3"];

function printStuff(a, b, c) {
  console.log("Printing: " + a + " " + b + " " + c);
}
```

```
// using the spread operator
printStuff(...items);
```

```
// without using the spread operator
printStuff(items[0], items[1], items[2]);
```

The situation we are facing with transferring properties across components is very similar to our problem of accessing each array item individually. Allow me to elaborate.

Inside a component, our `props` object looks as follows:

```
var props = {
  color: "steelblue",
  num: "3.14",
  size: "medium"
}
```

As part of passing these property values to a child component, we manually access each item from our `props` object:

```
<Display color={this.props.color}
         num={this.props.num}
         size={this.props.size}/>
```

Wouldn't it be great if there was a way to unwrap an object and pass on the property/value pairs just like we were able to unwrap an array using the spread operator?

As it turns out, there is a way. It actually involves the spread operator as well. I'll explain how later, but what this means is that we can call our `Display` component by using ...props:

```
<Display {...props}/>
```

By using ...props, the runtime behavior is the same as specifying the `color`, `num`, and `size` properties manually. This means our earlier example can be simplified as follows (pay attention to the highlighted lines):

```
var Display = React.createClass({
  render: function() {
    return(
      <div>
        <p>{this.props.color}</p>
        <p>{this.props.num}</p>
        <p>{this.props.size}</p>
      </div>
    );
  }
});


var Label = React.createClass({
  render: function() {
    return (
```

```
        <Display {...this.props}/>
    );
  }
});

var Shirt = React.createClass({
  render: function() {
      return (
        <div>
          <Label {...this.props}/>
        </div>
      );
    }
});

ReactDOM.render(
  <div>
    <Shirt color="steelblue" num="3.14" size="medium"/>
  </div>,
  document.querySelector("#container")
);
```

If you run this code, the end result is going to be unchanged from what we had earlier. The biggest difference is that we are no longer passing in expanded forms of each property as part of calling each component. This solves all the problems we originally set out to solve.

By using the spread operator, if you ever decide to add properties, rename properties, remove properties, or do any other sort of property-related shenanigans, you don't have to make a billion different changes. You make one change at the spot where you define your property. You make another change at the spot you consume the property. That's it. All of the intermediate components that merely transfer the properties on will remain untouched, for the {...this.props} expression contains no details of what goes on inside it.

Conclusion

As designed by the ES6/ES2015 committee, the spread operator is designed to work only on arrays and array-like creatures (aka that which has a Symbol.iterator property). The fact that it works on object literals like our props object is due to React extending the standard. As of now, no browser currently supports using the spread object on object literals. The reason our example works is because of Babel. Besides turning all of our JSX into something our browser understands, Babel also turns cutting-edge and experimental features into something cross-browser friendly. That is why we are able to get away with using the spread operator on an object literal, and that is why we are able to elegantly solve the problem of transferring properties across multiple layers of components!

7

Meet JSX—Again!

As you probably noticed by now, we've been using a lot of JSX in the previous chapters. What we really haven't done is taken a good look at what JSX actually is. How does it actually work? Why do we not just call it HTML? What quirks does it have up its sleeve? In this chapter, we answer all of those questions and more! We do some serious backtracking (and some forwardtracking!) to get a deeper look at what we need to know about JSX in order to be dangerous.

What Happens with JSX?

One of the biggest things we've glossed over is trying to figure out what happens with our JSX after we've written it. How does it end up as HTML that we see in our browser? Take a look at the following example where we define a component called Card:

```
var Card = React.createClass({
  render: function() {
      var cardStyle = {
        height: 200,
        width: 150,
        padding: 0,
        backgroundColor: "#FFF",
        WebkitFilter: "drop-shadow(0px 0px 5px #666)",
        filter: "drop-shadow(0px 0px 5px #666)"
      };

      return (
        <div style={cardStyle}>
          <Square color={this.props.color}/>
          <Label color={this.props.color}/>
        </div>
      );
    }
});
```

We can quickly spot the JSX here. It is the following four lines:

```
<div style={cardStyle}>
  <Square color={this.props.color}/>
  <Label color={this.props.color}/>
</div>
```

The thing to keep in mind is that our browsers have no idea what to do with JSX. They probably think you are crazy if you ever even try to describe JSX to them. That is why we have been relying on things like Babel to turn that JSX into something the browsers understand: **JavaScript**.

What this means is that the JSX we write is for human (and well-trained cats') eyes only. When this JSX reaches our browser, it ends up getting turned into pure JavaScript:

```
return React.createElement(
  "div",
  { style: cardStyle },
  React.createElement(Square, { color: this.props.color }),
  React.createElement(Label, { color: this.props.color })
);
```

All of those neatly nested HTML-like elements, their attributes, and their children all get turned into a series of `createElement` calls with default initialization values. Here is what our entire `Card` component looks like when it gets turned into JavaScript:

```
var Card = React.createClass({
  displayName: "Card",

  render: function render() {
    var cardStyle = {
      height: 200,
      width: 150,
      padding: 0,
      backgroundColor: "#FFF",
      WebkitFilter: "drop-shadow(0px 0px 5px #666)",
      filter: "drop-shadow(0px 0px 5px #666)"
    };

    return React.createElement(
      "div",
      { style: cardStyle },
      React.createElement(Square, { color: this.props.color }),
      React.createElement(Label, { color: this.props.color })
    );
  }
});
```

Notice that there is no trace of JSX anywhere! All of these changes between what you wrote and what our browser sees are part of the transpiling step we've talked about in the first chapter. That transpilation is something that happens entirely behind-the-scenes thanks to Babel, which we've been to perform this JSX→JS transformation entirely in the browser. We'll eventually look at using Babel as part of a more-involved build environment where we will just generate a transformed JS file, but more on that when we get there in the future.

But yeah, there you have it. An answer to what exactly happens to all of our JSX. It gets turned into sweet SWEET JavaScript.

JSX Quirks to Remember

As we've been working with JSX, you probably noticed that we ran into some arbitrary rules and exceptions to what you can and can't do. In this section, let's put all of those quirks together in one area and maybe even run into some brand new ones!

You Can Only Return A Single Root Node

This is probably the first quirk we ran into. In JSX, what you return or render can't be made up of multiple root elements:

```
ReactDOM.render(
  <Letter>B</Letter>
  <Letter>E</Letter>
  <Letter>I</Letter>
  <Letter>O</Letter>
  <Letter>U</Letter>,
  document.querySelector("#container")
);
```

If you want to do something like this, you need to wrap all of your elements into a single parent element first:

```
ReactDOM.render(
  <div>
    <Letter>A</Letter>
    <Letter>E</Letter>
    <Letter>I</Letter>
    <Letter>O</Letter>
    <Letter>U</Letter>
  </div>,
  document.querySelector("#container")
);
```

This seemed like a bizarre requirement when we looked at it before, but you can blame `createElement` for why we do this. With the `render` and `return` functions, what you are ultimately returning is a single `createElement` call (which in turn might have many nested `createElement` calls). Here is what our earlier JSX looks like when turned into JavaScript:

```
ReactDOM.render(React.createElement(
  "div",
  null,
  React.createElement(
    Letter,
    null,
    "A"
  ),
  React.createElement(
    Letter,
    null,
    "E"
  ),
  React.createElement(
    Letter,
    null,
    "I"
  ),
  React.createElement(
    Letter,
    null,
    "O"
  ),
  React.createElement(
    Letter,
    null,
    "U"
  )
), document.querySelector("#container"));
```

Having multiple root elements would break how functions return values and how `createElement` works, so that is why you can specify only one return (root) element! You can now sleep better knowing this.

You Can't Specify CSS Inline

As we saw in Chapter 4, the `style` attribute in your JSX behaves differently from the `style` attribute in HTML. In HTML, you can specify CSS properties directly as values on your `style` attribute:

```
<div style="font-family:Arial;font-size:24px">
    <p>Blah!</p>
</div>
```

In JSX, the `style` attribute can't contain CSS inside it. Instead, it needs to refer to an object that contains styling information instead:

```
var Letter = React.createClass({
  render: function() {
      var letterStyle = {
        padding: 10,
        margin: 10,
        backgroundColor: this.props.bgcolor,
        color: "#333",
        display: "inline-block",
        fontFamily: "monospace",
        fontSize: "32",
        textAlign: "center"
      };

      return (
        <div style={letterStyle}>
          {this.props.children}
        </div>
      );
    }
});
```

Notice that we have an object called `letterStyle` that that contains all of the CSS properties (in camelcase JavaScript form) and their values. That object is what we then specify to the `style` attribute.

Reserved Keywords and `className`

JavaScript has a bunch of keywords and values that you can't use as identifiers. Those keywords currently (as of ES2016) are:

break	case	class	catch	const	continue
debugger	default	delete	do	else	export
extends	finally	for	function	if	import
in	instanceof	new	return	super	switch
this	throw	try	typeof	var	void
while	with	yield			

When you are writing JSX, you should be careful to not use these keywords as part of any identifiers that you create as well. That can be difficult when certain really popular keywords like `class` are commonly used in HTML despite also being in JavaScript's reserved keywords list.

Take a look at the following:

```
ReactDOM.render(
  <div class="slideIn">
    <p class="emphasis">Gabagool!</p>
    <Label/>
  </div>,
  document.querySelector("#container")
);
```

Ignoring JavaScript's reservations about `class` (like what we've done here) won't work. What you need to do is use the DOM API version of the `class` attribute called `className` instead:

```
ReactDOM.render(
  <div className="slideIn">
    <p className="emphasis">Gabagool!</p>
    <Label/>
  </div>,
  document.querySelector("#container")
);
```

You can see the full list of supported tags and attributes at the following Facebook article (https://facebook.github.io/react/docs/tags-and-attributes.html), and *notice that all of the attributes are camelcase*. That detail is important, for using the lowercase version of an attribute won't work. If you are ever pasting a large chunk of HTML that you want JSX to deal with, be sure to go back to your pasted HTML and make these minor adjustments to turn it into valid JSX.

This brings up another point. Because of these minor deviations from HTML behavior, we tend to say that JSX supports an *HTML-like syntax* as opposed to just saying that JSX supports HTML. This is a deliberate React-ism. The clearest answer to the relationship between JSX and HTML comes from React team member, Ben Alpert, who stated the following (http://qr.ae/RUKaON) as part of a Quora answer:

> ...our thinking is that JSX's primary advantage is the symmetry of matching closing tags which makes [sic] code easier to read, not the direct resemblance to HTML or XML. It's convenient to copy/paste HTML directly, but other minor differences (in self-closing tags, for example) make this a losing battle and we have a HTML to JSX converter to help you anyway. Finally, to translate HTML to idiomatic React code, a fair amount of work is usually involved in breaking up the markup into components that make sense, so changing `class` to `className` is only a small part of that anyway.

Comments

Just like it is a good idea to comment your HTML, CSS, and JavaScript, it is a good idea to provide comments inside your JSX as well. Specifying comments in JSX is very similar to how you would comment in JavaScript (https://www.kirupa.com/html5/comments.htm) ...except for one exception. If you are specifying a comment as a child of a tag, you need to wrap your comment by the { and } curly brackets to ensure it is parsed as an expression:

```
ReactDOM.render(
  <div class="slideIn">
    <p class="emphasis">Gabagool!</p>
    {/* I am a child comment */}
    <Label/>
  </div>,
  document.querySelector("#container")
);
```

Our comment in this case is a child of our div element. If you specify a comment wholly inside a tag, you can just specify your single-or multi-line comment without having to use the { and } angle brackets:

```
ReactDOM.render(
  <div class="slideIn">
    <p class="emphasis">Gabagool!</p>
    <Label
      /* This comment
         goes across
         multiple lines */
         className="colorCard" // end of line
    />
  </div>,
  document.querySelector("#container")
);
```

In this snippet, you can see an example of what both multi-line comments and a comment at the end of a line look like. Now that you know all of this, you have one less excuse to not comment your JSX :P

Capitalization, HTML Elements, and Components

Capitalization is important. To represent HTML elements, ensure the HTML tag is lower-case:

```
ReactDOM.render(
  <div>
    <section>
      <p>Something goes here!</p>
    </section>
  </div>,
  document.querySelector("#container")
);
```

When wishing to represent components, the component name must be capitalized, both in JSX as well as when you define them:

```
ReactDOM.render(
  <div>
    <MyCustomComponent/>
```

```
  </div>,
  document.querySelector("#container")
);
```

If you get the capitalization wrong, React will not render your content properly. The component will not be found. Trying to identify capitalization issues is probably the last thing you'll think about when things aren't working, so keep this little tip in mind.

Your JSX Can Be Anywhere

In many situations, your JSX will not be neatly arranged inside a `render` or `return` function like in the examples we've seen so far. Take a look at the following example:

```
var swatchComponent = <Swatch color="#2F004F"></Swatch>;
```

```
ReactDOM.render(
  <div>
    {swatchComponent}
  </div>,
  document.querySelector("#container")
);
```

We have a variable called `swatchComponent` that is initialized to a line of JSX. When our `swatchComponent` variable is placed inside the render function, our `Swatch` component gets initialized. All of this is totally valid, and we will do more such things in the future when we learn how to generate and manipulate JSX using JavaScript.

Conclusion

With this chapter, we've finally pieced together in one location the various bits of JSX information that the previous chapters introduced. The most important thing to remember is that *JSX is not HTML*. It looks like HTML and behaves like it in many common scenarios, but it is ultimately designed to be translated into JavaScript. This means you can do things that you could never imagine doing using just plain HTML. Being able to evaluate expressions or programmatically manipulate entire chunks of JSX is just the beginning. In upcoming chapters, we'll explore this intersection of JavaScript and JSX further.

8

Dealing with State

Up until this point, the components we've created have been stateless. They have properties (aka props) that are passed in from their parent, but nothing (usually) changes about them once the components come alive. Your properties are considered immutable once they have been set. For many interactive scenarios, you don't want that. You want to be able to change aspects of your components as a result of some user interaction (or some data getting returned from a server or a billion other things!)

What we need is another way to store data on a component that goes beyond properties. We need a way to store data that can be changed. What we need is something known as **state**! In this chapter you learn all about it and how you can use it to create stateful components.

Using State

If you know how to work with properties, you totally know how to work with states... sort of. There are some differences, but they are too subtle to bore you with right now. Instead, let's just jump right in and see states in action by using them in a small example.

What we are going to is create a simple lightning counter example as shown in Figure 8-1.

Figure 8-1   The app you will be building.

What this example does is nothing crazy. Lightning strikes the earth's surface about 100 times a second (http://environment.nationalgeographic.com/environment/natural-disasters/lightning-profile/). We have a counter that simply increments a number you see by that same amount. Let's create it.

Our Starting Point

The primary focus of this example is to see how we can work with state. There is no point in us spending a bunch of time creating the example from scratch and retracing paths that we've walked many times already. That's not the best use of anybody's time.

Instead of starting from scratch, modify an existing HTML document or create a new one with the following contents:

```
<!DOCTYPE html>
<html>

<head>
  <title>More State!</title>
  <script src="https://unpkg.com/react@15.3.2/dist/react.js"></script>
  <script src="https://unpkg.com/react-dom@15.3.2/dist/react-dom.js"></script>
  <script src="https://cdnjs.cloudflare.com/ajax/libs/babel-core/5.8.23/browser.min
.js"></script>
</head>
```

```
<body>
  <div id="container"></div>
  <script type="text/babel">
    var LightningCounter = React.createClass({
      render: function() {
        return (
          <h1>Hello!</h1>
        );
      }
    });

    var LightningCounterDisplay = React.createClass({
      render: function() {

        var divStyle = {
          width: 250,
          textAlign: "center",
          backgroundColor: "black",
          padding: 40,
          fontFamily: "sans-serif",
          color: "#999",
          borderRadius: 10
        };

        return(
          <div style={divStyle}>
            <LightningCounter/>
          </div>
        );
      }
    });

    ReactDOM.render(
      <LightningCounterDisplay/>,
      document.querySelector("#container")
    );
  </script>
</body>

</html>
```

At this point, take a few moments to look at what our existing code does. First, we have a component called `LightningCounterDisplay`:

```
var LightningCounterDisplay = React.createClass({
    render: function() {
```

```
  var divStyle = {
    width: 250,
    textAlign: "center",
    backgroundColor: "black",
    padding: 40,
    fontFamily: "sans-serif",
    color: "#999",
    borderRadius: 10
  };

  return(
    <div style={divStyle}>
      <LightningCounter/>
    </div>
  );
  }
});
```

The bulk of this component is the `divStyle` object that contains the styling information responsible for the cool rounded background. The `render` function returns a `div` element that wraps the `LightningCounter` component.

The `LightningCounter` component is where all the action is going to be taking place:

```
var LightningCounter = React.createClass({
  render: function() {
    return (
      <h1>Hello!</h1>
    );
  }
});
```

This component, as it is right now, has nothing interesting going for it. It just returns the word **Hello!** That's OK—we'll fix this component up later.

The last thing to look at is our `ReactDOM.render` method:

```
ReactDOM.render(
  <LightningCounterDisplay/>,
  document.querySelector("#container")
);
```

It just pushes the `LightningCounterDisplay` component into our **container** div element in our DOM. That's pretty much it. The end result is that you see the combination of markup from our `ReactDOM.render` method and the `LightningCounterDisplay` and `LightningCounter` components.

Getting Our Counter On

Now that we have an idea of what we are starting with, it's time to make plans for our next steps. The way our counter works is pretty simple. We are going to be using a `setInterval` function that calls some code every 1000 milliseconds (aka 1 second). That "some code" is going to increment a value by **100** each time it is called. Seems pretty straightforward, right?

To make this all work, we are going to be relying on three APIs that our React Component exposes:

- `getInitialState`–This method runs just *before* your component gets mounted, and it allows you to modify a component's `state` object.

- `componentDidMount`–This method gets called just *after* our component gets rendered (or **mounted** as React calls it).

- `setState`–This method allows you to update the value of the `state` object.

We'll see these APIs in use shortly, but I wanted to give you a preview of them so that you can spot them easily in a lineup!

Setting the Initial State Value

We need a variable to act as our counter, and let's call this variable `strikes`. There are a bunch of ways to create this variable. The most obvious one is the following:

```
var strikes = 0 // :P
```

We don't want to do that, though. For our example, the `strikes` variable is part of our component's state, and its value is what we display on screen. What we are going to do is use the `getInitialState` method that we briefly saw a few moments ago and take care of initializing our variable inside it. You'll see in a few moments what result that has on our component's state.

Inside your `LightningCounter` component, add the following highlighted lines:

```
var LightningCounter = React.createClass({
  getInitialState: function() {
    return {
      strikes: 0
    };
  },
  render: function() {
    return (
      <h1>{this.state.strikes}</h1>
    );
  }
});
```

The `getInitialState` method automatically runs waaaay before your component gets rendered, and what we are doing is telling React to return an object containing our `strikes` property (initialized to 0). You may be wondering to whom or what we are returning this object to? All of that is magic that happens under the covers. *The object that gets returned is set as the initial value for our component's* `state` *object.*

If we inspect the value of our `state` object after this code has run, it would look something like the following:

```
var state = {
  strikes: 0
}
```

Before we wrap this section up, let's visualize our `strikes` property. In our `render` method, make the following highlighted change:

```
var LightningCounter = React.createClass({
  getInitialState: function() {
    return {
      strikes: 0
    };
  },
  render: function() {
    return (
      <h1>{this.state.strikes}</h1>
    );
  }
});
```

What we've done is replaced our default **Hello!** text with an expression that displays the value stored by the `this.state.strikes` property. If you preview your example in the browser, you will see a value of 0 displayed. That's a start!

Starting Our Timer and Setting State

Next up is getting our timer going and incrementing our `strikes` property. Like we mentioned earlier, we will be using the `setInterval` function to increase the `strikes` property by **100** every second. We are going to do all of this immediately after our component has been rendered using the built-in `componentDidMount` method.

The code for kicking off our timer looks as follows:

```
var LightningCounter = React.createClass({
  getInitialState: function() {
    return {
      strikes: 0
    };
  },
```

```
  componentDidMount: function() {
    setInterval(this.timerTick, 1000);
  },
  render: function() {
    return (
      <h1>{this.state.strikes}</h1>
    );
  }
});
```

Go ahead and add these highlighted lines to our example. Inside our componentDidMount method that gets called once, our component gets rendered, we have our setInterval method that calls a timerTick function every second (or 1000 milliseconds).

We haven't defined our timerTick function, so let's fix that by adding the following highlighted lines to our code:

```
var LightningCounter = React.createClass({
  getInitialState: function() {
    return {
      strikes: 0
    };
  },
  timerTick: function() {
    this.setState({
      strikes: this.state.strikes + 100
    });
  },
  componentDidMount: function() {
    setInterval(this.timerTick, 1000);
  },
  render: function() {
    return (
      <h1>{this.state.strikes}</h1>
    );
  }
});
```

What our timerTick function does is pretty simple. It just calls setState. The setState method comes in various flavors, but for what we are doing here, it just takes an object as its argument. This object contains all the properties you want to *merge into the state object*. In our case, we are specifying the strikes property and setting its value to be 100 more than what it is currently.

How does timerTick maintain context?

In regular JavaScript, the timerTick function won't maintain context. You have to do extra work to support that. The reason it works in the React world is because of something known as **autobinding**. Now, aren't you glad you know that?

Rendering the State Change

If you preview your app now, you'll see our `strikes` value start to increment by 100 every second (see Figure 8-2).

Figure 8-2   The `strikes` value increments by 100 every second.

Let's ignore for a moment what happens with our code. That is pretty straightforward. The interesting thing is how everything we've done ends up updating what you see on the screen. That updating has to do with this React behavior: *Whenever you call* `setState` *and update something in the* `state` *object, your component's* `render` *method gets automatically called.* This kicks off a cascade of `render` calls for any component whose output is also affected. The end result of all this is that what you see in your screen in the latest representation of your app's UI state. Keeping your data and UI in sync is one of the hardest problems with UI development, so it's nice that React takes care of this for us. It makes all of this pain of learning to use React totally worth it—almost! :P

Optional: The Full Code

What we have right now is just a counter that increments by 100 every second. Nothing about it screams *Lightning Counter*, but it does cover everything about states that I wanted you to learn right now. If you want to optionally flesh out your example to look like my version that you saw at the beginning, below is the full code for what goes inside our `script` tag:

```
var LightningCounter = React.createClass({
  getInitialState: function() {
    return {
      strikes: 0
    };
  },
  timerTick: function() {
    this.setState({
      strikes: this.state.strikes + 100
    });
  },
```

```
  componentDidMount: function() {
    setInterval(this.timerTick, 1000);
  },
  render: function() {
    var counterStyle = {
      color: "#66FFFF",
      fontSize: 50
    };

    var count = this.state.strikes.toLocaleString();

    return (
      <h1 style={counterStyle}>{count}</h1>
    );
  }
});

var LightningCounterDisplay = React.createClass({
    render: function() {
      var commonStyle = {
        margin: 0,
        padding: 0
      }
      var divStyle = {
        width: 250,
        textAlign: "center",
        backgroundColor: "#020202",
        padding: 40,
        fontFamily: "sans-serif",
        color: "#999999",
        borderRadius: 10
      };

      var textStyles = {
        emphasis: {
          fontSize: 38,
          ...commonStyle
        },
        smallEmphasis: {
          ...commonStyle
        },
        small: {
          fontSize: 17,
          opacity: 0.5,
          ...commonStyle
        }
      }
```

```
      return(
        <div style={divStyle}>
          <LightningCounter/>
          <h2 style={textStyles.smallEmphasis}>LIGHTNING STRIKES</h2>
          <h2 style={textStyles.emphasis}>WORLDWIDE</h2>
          <p style={textStyles.small}>(since you loaded this example)</p>
        </div>
      );
    }
});

ReactDOM.render(
  <LightningCounterDisplay/>,
  document.querySelector("#container")
);
```

If you make your code look like everything you see above and run the example again, you will see our lightning counter example in all its cyan-colored glory. While you are at it, take a moment to look through the code to ensure you don't see too many surprises.

Conclusion

We just scratched the surface on what we can do to create stateful components. While using a timer to update something in our state object is cool, the real action happens when we start combining user interaction with state. So far, we've shied away from the large amount of mouse, touch, keyboard, and other related things that your components will come into contact with. In an upcoming chapter, we are going to fix that. Along the way, you'll see us taking what we've seen about states to a whole new level! If that doesn't excite you, then I don't know what will :P

9

Going from Data to UI

When you are building your apps, thinking in terms of props, state, components, JSX tags, `render` methods, and other React-isms may be the last thing on your mind. Most of the time, you are dealing with data in the form of JSON objects, arrays, and other data structures that have no knowledge (or interest) in React or anything visual. Bridging the gulf between your data and what you eventually see can be frustrating! Not to worry, though. This chapter helps reduce some of those frustrating moments by running through some common scenarios you'll encounter!

The Example

To help make sense of everything you are about to see, we are going to need an example. It's nothing too complicated, so go ahead and create a new HTML document and throw the following stuff into it:

```
<!DOCTYPE html>
<html>

<head>
  <title>React! React! React!</title>
  <script src="https://unpkg.com/react@15.3.2/dist/react.js"></script>
  <script src="https://unpkg.com/react-dom@15.3.2/dist/react-dom.js"></script>
  <script src="https://cdnjs.cloudflare.com/ajax/libs/babel-core/5.8.23/browser.min
.js"></script>

  <style>
    #container {
      padding: 50px;
      background-color: #FFF;
    }
  </style>
</head>
```

```
<body>
  <div id="container"></div>
  <script type="text/babel">
    var Circle = React.createClass({
      render: function() {
        var circleStyle = {
          padding: 10,
          margin: 20,
          display: "inline-block",
          backgroundColor: this.props.bgColor,
          borderRadius: "50%",
          width: 100,
          height: 100,
        };

        return (
          <div style={circleStyle}>
          </div>
        );
      }
    });

    var destination = document.querySelector("#container");

    ReactDOM.render(
      <div>
        <Circle bgColor="#F9C240"/>
      </div>,
      destination
    );
  </script>
</body>

</html>
```

Once you have your document set up, go ahead and preview what you have in your browser.
If everything went well, you will be greeted by a happy yellow circle (see Figure 9-1).

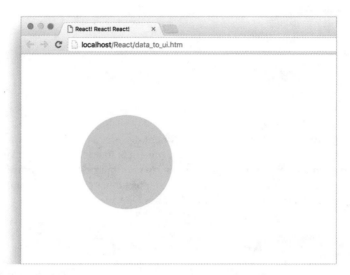

Figure 9-1   If everything went well, you will get this yellow circle.

If you see what I see, great! Now, let's take a moment to understand what our example is doing. The bulk of what you see comes from the `Circle` component:

```
var Circle = React.createClass({
  render: function() {
     var circleStyle = {
        padding: 10,
        margin: 20,
        display: "inline-block",
        backgroundColor: this.props.bgColor,
        borderRadius: "50%",
        width: 100,
        height: 100,
     };

     return (
       <div style={circleStyle}>
       </div>
     );
   }
});
```

It is mostly made up of our `circleStyle` object that contains the inline style properties that turn our boring `div` into an awesome circle. All the style values are hard-coded except for the `backgroundColor` property. It takes its value from the `bgColor` prop that gets passed in.

Going beyond our component, the way we ultimately display our circle is via our usual `ReactDOM.render` method:

```
ReactDOM.render(
  <div>
    <Circle bgColor="#F9C240"/>
  </div>,
  destination
);
```

We have a single instance of our `Circle` component declared, and we declare it with the `bgColor` prop set to the color we want our circle to appear in. Now, having our `Circle` component be defined as-is inside our render method is a bit limiting - especially if you are going to be dealing with data that could affect what our `Circle` component does. In the next couple of sections, we'll look at the ways we have for solving that.

Your JSX Can Be Anywhere—Part II

In the "Meet JSX—Again"! chapter (Chapter 7), we learned that our JSX can actually live outside of a render function and can be used as a value assigned to a variable or property. For example, we can fearlessly do something like this:

```
var theCircle = <Circle bgColor="#F9C240"/>;

ReactDOM.render(
  <div>
    {theCircle}
  </div>,
  destination
);
```

The `theCircle` variable stores the JSX for instantiating our `Circle` component. Evaluating this variable inside our `ReactDOM.render` function results in a circle getting displayed. The end result is no different than what we had earlier, but having our `Circle` component instantiation freed from the shackles of the `render` method gives us more options to do crazy and cool things.

For example, you can go further and create a function that returns a `Circle` component:

```
function showCircle() {
  var colors = ["#393E41", "#E94F37", "#1C89BF", "#A1D363"];
  var ran = Math.floor(Math.random() * colors.length);

  // return a Circle with a randomly chosen color
  return <Circle bgColor={colors[ran]}/>;
};
```

In this case, the showCircle function returns a Circle component (boring!) with the value for the bgColor prop set to a random color value (awesomesauce!). To have our example use the showCircle function, all you have to do is evaluate it inside ReactDOM.render:

```
1  ReactDOM.render(
2    <div>
3      {showCircle()}
4    </div>,
5    destination
6  );
```

As long as the expression you are evaluating returns JSX, you can put pretty much anything you want inside the { and } curly brackets. That flexibility is really nice, because there are a lot of things you can do when your JavaScript lives outside of the render function. A LOT OF THINGS!

Dealing with Arrays in the Context of JSX

Now we are going to get to some fun stuff! When you are displaying multiple components, you won't always be able to manually specify them:

```
ReactDOM.render(
  <div>
    {showCircle()}
    {showCircle()}
    {showCircle()}
  </div>,
  destination
);
```

In many real-world scenarios, the number of components you display will be related to the number of items in an array or array-like (aka iterator) object you are working with. That brings along a few simple complications. For example, let's say that we have an array called colors that looks as follows:

```
var colors = ["#393E41", "#E94F37", "#1C89BF", "#A1D363",
              "#85FFC7", "#297373", "#FF8552", "#A40E4C"];
```

What we want to do is create a Circle component for each item in this array (and set the bgColor prop to the value of each array item). The way we are going to do this is by creating an array of Circle components:

```
var colors = ["#393E41", "#E94F37", "#1C89BF", "#A1D363",
              "#85FFC7", "#297373", "#FF8552", "#A40E4C"];

var renderData = [];

for (var i = 0; i < colors.length; i++) {
  renderData.push(<Circle bgColor={colors[i]}/>);
}
```

In this snippet, we populate our `renderData` array with `Circle` components just like we originally set out to do. So far so good. To display all of these components, React makes it very simple. Take a look at the highlighted line for all you have to do:

```
var colors = ["#393E41", "#E94F37", "#1C89BF", "#A1D363",
              "#85FFC7", "#297373", "#FF8552", "#A40E4C"];

var renderData = [];

for (var i = 0; i < colors.length; i++) {
  renderData.push(<Circle bgColor={colors[i]}/>);
}

ReactDOM.render(
  <div>
    {renderData}
  </div>,
  destination
);
```

In our `render` method, all we do is specify our `renderData` array as an expression that we need to evaluate. We don't need to take any other step to go from an array of components to seeing something that looks like Figure 9-2 when you preview in your browser.

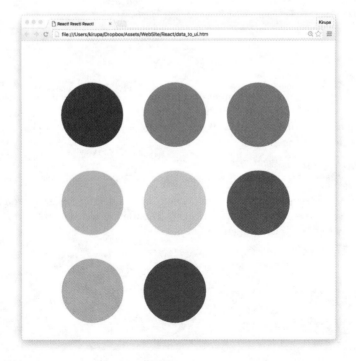

Figure 9-2   What you should see in your browser.

Ok, while our example seems to work, we aren't done yet! There is actually one more thing we need to do, and this is a subtle one. The way React makes UI updates really fast is by having a good idea of what exactly is going on in your DOM. It does this in several ways, but one really noticeable way is by internally marking each element with some sort of an identifier. This "marking" happens automatically when you explicitly specify elements in your JSX.

When you create elements dynamically (such as what we are doing with our array of `Circle` components), these identifiers are not automatically set. We need to do some extra work. That extra work takes the form of a `key` prop whose value React uses to uniquely identify each particular component.

For our example, we can do something like this:

```
for (var i = 0; i < colors.length; i++) {
  var color = colors[i];
  renderData.push(<Circle key={i + color} bgColor={color}/>);
}
```

On each component, we specify our `key` prop and set its value to a combination of color and index position inside the `colors` array. This ensures that each component we dynamically create ends up getting a unique identifier that React can then use to optimize any future UI updates. Now, we could just use the index position as the identifier, but if you have multiple blocks of code where you are dynamically generating elements, you may get multiple elements with duplicate index values.

> **Check Your Console Yo!**
>
> React is really good at telling you when you might be doing something wrong. For example, if you dynamically create elements or components and don't specify a `key` prop on them, you will be greeted with the following warning in your console:
>
> **Warning: Each child in an array or iterator should have a unique "key" prop. Check the top-level render call using <div>.**
>
> When you are working with React, it is a good idea to periodically check your console for any messages it may have. Even if things seem to be working just fine, you'll never know what you might find :P

Conclusion

All the tips and tricks you've seen in this article are made possibly because of one thing: *JSX is JavaScript.* This is what enables you to have your JSX live wherever JavaScript thrives. To us, it looks like we are doing something absolutely bizarre when we specify something like this:

```
for (var i = 0; i < colors.length; i++) {
  var color = colors[i];
  renderData.push(<Circle key={i + color} bgColor={color}/>);
}
```

Even though we are pushing pieces of JSX to an array, just like magic, everything works in the end when `renderData` is evaluated inside our `render` method. I hate to sound like a broken record, but this is because what our browser ultimately sees looks like this:

```
for (var i = 0; i < colors.length; i++) {
  var color = colors[i];

  renderData.push(React.createElement(Circle,
    {
      key: i + color,
      bgColor: color
    }));
}
```

When our JSX gets converted into pure JS, everything makes sense again. This is what allows us to get away with putting our JSX in all sorts of uncomfortable (yet photogenic!) situations with our data and still get the end result we want! Because, in the end, it's all just JavaScript.

10

Working with Events

So far, most of our examples only did their work on page load. As you probably guessed, that isn't normal. In most apps, especially the kind of UI-heavy ones we will be building, there is going to be a ton of things the app does only as a reaction to something. That *something* could be triggered by a mouse click, a key press, window resize, or a whole bunch of other gestures and interactions. The glue that makes all of this possible is something known as **events**.

Now, you probably know all about events from your experience using them in the DOM world. (If you don't, then I suggest getting a quick refresher first: https://www.kirupa.com/html5/javascript_events.htm.) The way React deals with events is a bit different, and these differences can surprise you in various ways if you aren't paying close attention. Don't worry. That's why you have this book! We start off with a few simple examples and then gradually look at increasingly more bizarre, complex, and (yes!) boring things.

Listening and Reacting to Events

The easiest way to learn about events in React is to actually use them, and that's exactly what we are going to do! To help with this, we have a simple example made up of a counter that increments each time you click on a button. Initially, our example will look like Figure 10-1.

Figure 10-1   Our example.

Each time you click on the plus button, the counter value will increase by 1. After clicking the plus button a bunch of times, it will look sorta like Figure 10-2.

Figure 10-2   After clicking the plus button a bunch of times (23?).

Under the covers, the way this example works is pretty simple. Each time you click on the button, an event gets fired. We listen for this event and do all sorts of React-ey things to get the counter to update when this event gets overheard.

Starting Point

To save all of us some time, we aren't going to be creating everything in our example from scratch. By now, you probably have a good idea of how to work with components, styles, state, and so on. Instead, we are going to start off with a partially implemented example that contains everything except the event-related functionality that we are here to learn.

First, create a new HTML document and ensure your starting point looks as follows:

```html
<!DOCTYPE html>
<html>

<head>
  <title>React! React! React!</title>
  <script src="https://unpkg.com/react@15.3.2/dist/react.js"></script>
  <script src="https://unpkg.com/react-dom@15.3.2/dist/react-dom.js"></script>
  <script src="https://cdnjs.cloudflare.com/ajax/libs/babel-core/5.8.23/browser.min
.js"></script>

  <style>
    #container {
      padding: 50px;
      background-color: #FFF;
    }
```

```
    </style>
</head>

<body>
    <div id="container"></div>                    •
    <script type="text/babel">

    </script>
</body>

</html>
```

Once your new HTML document looks like what you see above, it's time to add our partially implemented counter example. Inside our script tag below the **container** div, add the following:

```
var destination = document.querySelector("#container");

var Counter = React.createClass({
  render: function() {
      var textStyle = {
        fontSize: 72,
        fontFamily: "sans-serif",
        color: "#333",
        fontWeight: "bold"
      };

      return (
        <div style={textStyle}>
          {this.props.display}
        </div>
      );
    }
});

var CounterParent = React.createClass({
  getInitialState: function() {
    return {
      count: 0
    };
  },
  render: function() {
      var backgroundStyle = {
        padding: 50,
        backgroundColor: "#FFC53A",
        width: 250,
        height: 100,
        borderRadius: 10,
        textAlign: "center"
      };
```

```
    var buttonStyle = {
      fontSize: "1em",
      width: 30,
      height: 30,
      fontFamily: "sans-serif",
      color: "#333",
      fontWeight: "bold",
      lineHeight: "3px"
    };

    return (
      <div style={backgroundStyle}>
        <Counter display={this.state.count}/>
        <button style={buttonStyle}>+</button>
      </div>
    );
  }
});

ReactDOM.render(
  <div>
    <CounterParent/>
  </div>,
  destination
);
```

Once you have added all of this, preview everything in your browser to make sure things get displayed. You should see the beginning of our counter. Take a few moments to look at what all of this code does. There shouldn't be anything that looks strange. The only odd thing will be that clicking the plus button won't do anything. We'll fix that right up in the next section.

Making the Button Click Do Something

Each time we click on the plus button, we want the value of our counter to increase by one. What we need to do is going to look roughly like this:

1. Listen for the click event on the button and specify an event handler.

2. Implement the event handler where we increase the value of our `this.state.count` property that our counter relies on.

We'll just go straight down the list—starting with listening for the click event. In React, you listen to an event by specifying everything inline in your JSX itself. More specifically, *you specify both the event you are listening for and the event handler that will get called, all inside your markup.*

To do this, find the `return` function inside our `CounterParent` component, and make the following highlighted change:

```
    .
    .
    .
return (
  <div style={backgroundStyle}>
    <Counter display={this.state.count}/>
    <button onClick={this.increase} style={buttonStyle}>+</button>
  </div>
);
```

What we've done is told React to call the `increase` function when the `onClick` event is overheard. Next, let's go ahead and implement the `increase` function—aka our event handler. Inside our `CounterParent` component, add the following highlighted lines:

```
var CounterParent = React.createClass({
  getInitialState: function() {
    return {
      count: 0
    };
  },
  increase: function(e) {
    this.setState({
      count: this.state.count + 1
    });
  },
  render: function() {
    var backgroundStyle = {
      padding: 50,
      backgroundColor: "#FFC53A",
      width: 250,
      height: 100,
      borderRadius: 10,
      textAlign: "center"
    };

    var buttonStyle = {
      fontSize: "1em",
      width: 30,
      height: 30,
      fontFamily: "sans-serif",
      color: "#333",
      fontWeight: "bold",
      lineHeight: "3px"
    };
```

```
      return (
        <div style={backgroundStyle}>
          <Counter display={this.state.count}/>
          <button onClick={this.increase} style={buttonStyle}>+</button>
        </div>
      );
    }
});
```

All we are doing with these lines is making sure that each call to the `increase` function increments the value of our `this.state.count` property by 1. Because we are dealing with events, your `increase` function (as the designated event handler) will get access to the event argument. We have set this event argument to be accessed by `e`, and you can see that by looking at our `increase` function's signature (aka what its declaration looks like). We'll talk about the various events and their properties in a little bit.

Now, go ahead and preview what you have in your browser. Once everything has loaded, click on the plus button to see all of our newly added code in action. Our counter value should increase with each click! Isn't that pretty awesome?

Event Properties

As you know, our events pass what is known as an event argument to our event handler. This event argument contains a bunch of properties that are specific to the type of event you are dealing with. In the regular DOM world, each event has its own type. For example, if you are dealing with a mouse event, your event and its event argument object will be of type `MouseEvent`. This `MouseEvent` object will allow you to access mouse-specific information, like which button was pressed or the screen position of the mouse click. Event arguments for a keyboard-related event are of type `KeyboardEvent`. Your `KeyboardEvent` object contains properties which (among many other things) allow you to figure out which key was actually pressed. I could go on forever for every other `Event` type, but you get the point. Each `Event` type contains its own set of properties that you can access via the event handler for that event!

Why am I boring you with things you already know? Well...

Meet Synthetic Events

In React, when you specify an event in JSX like we did with `onClick`, you are not directly dealing with regular DOM events. Instead, you are dealing with a React-specific event type known as a `SyntheticEvent`. Your event handlers don't get native event arguments of type `MouseEvent`, `KeyboardEvent`, etc. They always get event arguments of type `SyntheticEvent` that wrap your browser's native event instead. What is the fallout of this in our code? Surprisingly not a whole lot.

Each `SyntheticEvent` contains the following properties:

Property Name	Type
bubbles	boolean
cancelable	boolean
currentTarget	DOMEventTarget
defaultPrevented	boolean
eventPhase	number
isTrusted	boolean
nativeEvent	DOMEvent
preventDefault()	void
isDefaultPrevented()	boolean
isPropagationStopped	void
target	DOMEventTarget
timeStamp	number
type	string

These properties should seem pretty straightforward—and generic! The non-generic stuff depends on what type of native event our `SyntheticEvent` is wrapping. This means that a `SyntheticEvent` that wraps a `MouseEvent` will have access to mouse-specific properties such as the following:

```
boolean altKey
number button
number buttons
number clientX
number clientY
boolean ctrlKey
boolean getModifierState(key)
boolean metaKey
number pageX
number pageY
DOMEventTarget relatedTarget
number screenX
number screenY
boolean shiftKey
```

Similarly, a `SyntheticEvent` that wraps a `KeyboardEvent` will have access to these additional keyboard-related properties:

```
boolean altKey
number charCode
```

```
boolean ctrlKey
boolean getModifierState(key)
string key
number keyCode
string locale
number location
boolean metaKey
boolean repeat
boolean shiftKey
number which
```

In the end, all of this means that you still get the same functionality in the `SyntheticEvent` world that you had in the vanilla DOM world.

Now, here is something I learned the hard way. *Don't refer to traditional DOM event documentation when using Synthetic events and their properties.* Because the `SyntheticEvent` wraps your native DOM event, events and their properties may not map one-to-one. Some DOM events don't even exist in React. To avoid running into any issues, if you want to know the name of a `SyntheticEvent` or any of its properties, *refer to the* React Event System document (https://facebook.github.io/react/docs/events.html) *instead*.

Doing Stuff With Event Properties

By now, you've probably seen more about the DOM and `SyntheticEvent` stuff than you'd probably like. To wash away the taste of all that text, let's write some code and put all of this newfound knowledge to good use. Right now, our counter example increments by one each time you click on the plus button. What we want to do is *increment our counter by ten when the Shift key on the keyboard is pressed* while clicking the plus button with our mouse.

The way we are going to do that is by using the `shiftKey` property that exists on the `SyntheticEvent` when using the mouse:

```
boolean altKey
number button
number buttons
number clientX
number clientY
boolean ctrlKey
boolean getModifierState(key)
boolean metaKey
number pageX
number pageY
DOMEventTarget relatedTarget
number screenX
number screenY
boolean shiftKey
```

The way this property works is simple. If the Shift key is pressed when this mouse event fires, then the `shiftKey` property value is **true**. Otherwise, the `shiftKey` property value is **false**. To increment our counter by 10 when the Shift key is pressed, go back to our `increase` function and make the following highlighted changes:

```
increase: function(e) {
  var currentCount = this.state.count;

  if (e.shiftKey) {
    currentCount += 10;
  } else {
    currentCount += 1;
  }

  this.setState({
    count: currentCount
  });
},
```

Once you've made the changes, preview our example in the browser. Each time you click on the plus button, your counter will increment by one just like it had always done. If you click on the plus button with your Shift key pressed, notice that our counter increments by 10 instead.

The reason that all of this works is because we change our incrementing behavior depending on whether the Shift key is pressed or not. That is primarily handled by the following lines:

```
if (e.shiftKey) {
  currentCount += 10;
} else {
  currentCount += 1;
}
```

If the `shiftKey` property on our `SyntheticEvent` event argument is **true**, we increment our counter by 10. If the `shiftKey` value is **false**, we just increment by 1.

More Eventing Shenanigans

We are not done yet! Up until this point, we've looked at how to work with events in React in a very simplistic way. In the real world, rarely will things be as direct as what we've seen. Your real apps will be more complex, and because React insists on doing things differently, we'll need to learn (or re-learn) some new event-related tricks and techniques to make our apps work. That's where this section comes in. We are going to look at some common situations you'll run into and how to deal with them.

You Can't Directly Listen to Events on Components

Let's say your component is nothing more than a button or another type of UI element that users will be interacting with. You can't get away with doing something like what we see in the following highlighted line:

```
var CounterParent = React.createClass({
  getInitialState: function() {
    return {
      count: 0
    };
  },
  increase: function() {
    this.setState({
      count: this.state.count + 1
    });
  },
  render: function() {
    return (
      <div>
        <Counter display={this.state.count}/>
        <PlusButton onClick={this.increase}/>
      </div>
    );
  }
});
```

On the surface, this line of JSX looks totally valid. When somebody clicks on our PlusButton component, the increase function will get called. In case you are curious, this is what our PlusButton component looks like:

```
var PlusButton = React.createClass({
  render: function() {
    return (
      <button>
        +
      </button>
    );
  }
});
```

Our PlusButton component doesn't do anything crazy. It only returns a single HTML element!

No matter how you slice and dice this, none of this matters. It doesn't matter how simple or obvious the HTML we are returning via a component looks like. *You simply can't listen for events on them directly.* The reason is because components are wrappers for DOM elements. What does it even mean to listen for an event on a component? Once your component gets unwrapped into DOM elements, does the outer HTML element act as the thing you are listening for the event on? Is it some other element? How do you distinguish between listening for an event and declaring a prop with a value?

There is no clear answer to any of those questions. It's too harsh to say that the solution is to simply not listen to events on components, either. Fortunately, there is a workaround where we treat the event handler as a prop and pass it on to the component. Inside the component, we can then assign the event to a DOM element and set the event handler to the the value of the prop we just passed in. I realize that probably makes no sense, so let's walk through an example.

Take a look at the following highlighted line:

```
var CounterParent = React.createClass({
  .
  .
  .
  render: function() {
    return (
      <div>
        <Counter display={this.state.count}/>
        <PlusButton clickHandler={this.increase}/>
      </div>
    );
  }
});
```

In this example, we create a property called `clickHandler` whose value is the `increase` event handler. Inside our `PlusButton` component, we can then do something like this:

```
var PlusButton = React.createClass({
  render: function() {
    return (
      <button onClick={this.props.clickHandler}>
        +
      </button>
    );
  }
});
```

On our `button` element, we specify the `onClick` event and set its value to the `clickHandler` prop. At runtime, this prop gets evaluated as our `increase` function, and clicking the plus button ensures the `increase` function gets called. This solves our problem while still allowing our component to participate in all this eventing goodness!

Listening to Regular DOM Events

If you thought the previous section was a doozy, wait till you see what we have here. Not all DOM events have `SyntheticEvent` equivalents. It may seem like you can just add the `on` prefix and capitalize the event you are listening for when specifying it inline in your JSX:

```
var Something = React.createClass({
  handleMyEvent: function(e) {
    // do something
  },
```

```
render: function() {
    return (
        <div onMyWeirdEvent={this.handleMyEvent}>Hello!</div>
    );
    }
});
```

It doesn't work that way! For those events that aren't officially recognized by React, you have to use the traditional approach that uses `addEventListener` with a few extra hoops to jump through.

Take a look at the following section of code:

```
var Something = React.createClass({
    handleMyEvent: function(e) {
        // do something
    },
    componentDidMount: function() {
        window.addEventListener("someEvent", this.handleMyEvent);
    },
    componentWillUnmount: function() {
        window.removeEventListener("someEvent", this.handleMyEvent);
    },
    render: function() {
        return (
            <div>Hello!</div>
        );
    }
});
```

We have our `Something` component that listens for an event called `someEvent`. We start listening for this event under the `componentDidMount` method which is automatically called when our component gets rendered. The way we listen for our event is by using `addEventListener` and specifying both the event and the event handler to call:

```
var Something = React.createClass({
    handleMyEvent: function(e) {
        // do something
    },
    componentDidMount: function() {
        window.addEventListener("someEvent", this.handleMyEvent);
    },
    componentWillUnmount: function() {
        window.removeEventListener("someEvent", this.handleMyEvent);
    },
    render: function() {
        return (
            <div>Hello!</div>
        );
    }
});
```

That should be pretty straightforward. The only other thing you need to keep in mind is removing the event listener when the component is about to be destroyed. To do that, you can use the opposite of the componentDidMount method, the componentWillUnmount method. Inside that method, put your removeEventListener call to ensure no trace of our event listening takes place after our component goes away.

The Meaning of `this` Inside the Event Handler

When dealing with events in React, the value of this inside your event handler is different from what you would normally see in the non-React DOM world. In the non-React world, the value of this inside an event handler refers to the element that your event is listening on:

```
function doSomething(e) {
  console.log(this); //button element
}

var foo = document.querySelector("button");
foo.addEventListener("click", doSomething, false);
```

In the React world (when your components are created using React.createClass), the value of this inside your event handler always refers to the *component the event handler lives in*:

```
var CounterParent = React.createClass({
  getInitialState: function() {
    return {
      count: 0
    };
  },
  increase: function(e) {
    console.log(this); // CounterParent component

    this.setState({
      count: this.state.count + 1
    });
  },
  render: function() {
      return (
        <div>
          <Counter display={this.state.count}/>
          <button onClick={this.increase}>+</button>
        </div>
      );
    }
});
```

In this example, the value of this inside the increase event handler refers to the CounterParent component. It doesn't refer to the element that triggered the event. You get this behavior because React automatically binds all methods inside a component to this.

This autobinding behavior only applies when your component is created using `React.createClass`. If you are using ES6 classes to define your components, the value of `this` inside your event handler is going to be undefined unless you explicitly bind it yourself:

```
<button onClick={this.increase.bind(this)}>+</button>
```

There is no autobinding magic that happens with the new class syntax, so be sure to keep that in mind if you aren't using `React.createClass` to create your components.

React...Why? Why?!

Before we call it a day, let's use this time to talk about why React decided to deviate from how we've worked with events in the past. There are two reasons:

- Browser Compatibility
- Improved Performance

Let's elaborate on these two reasons a little bit.

Browser Compatibility

Event handling is one of those things that mostly works consistently in modern browsers, but once you go back to older browser versions, things get really bad really quickly. By wrapping all of the native events as an object of type `SyntheticEvent`, React frees you from dealing with event handling quirks that you would end up having to deal with otherwise.

Improved Performance

In complex UIs, the more event handlers you have, the more memory your app takes up. Manually dealing with that isn't difficult, but it is a bit tedious as you try to group events under a common parent. Sometimes, that just isn't possible. Sometimes, the hassle doesn't outweigh the benefits. What React does is pretty clever.

React never attaches event handlers to the DOM elements directly. *It uses one event handler at the root of your document* that is responsible for listening to all events and calling the appropriate event handler as necessary (see Figure 10-3).

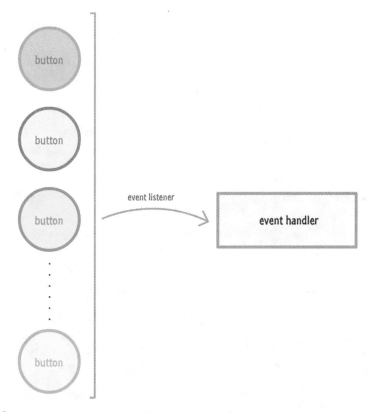

Figure 10-3   React uses one event handler at the root of your document.

This frees you from having to deal with optimizing your event handler-related code yourself. If you've manually had to do that in the past, you can relax knowing that React takes care of that tedious task for you. If you've never had to optimize event handler-related code yourself, consider yourself lucky :P

Conclusion

You'll spend a lot of time dealing with events, and this chapter threw a lot of things at you. We started by learning the basics of how to listen to events and specify the event handler. Towards the end, we were fully invested and looking at eventing corner cases that you will bump into if you aren't careful enough. You don't want to bump into corners. That is never fun.

11

The Component Lifecycle

In the beginning, we started off with a very simple view of components and what they do. As we learned more about React and did cooler and more involved things, it turns out our components aren't all that simple. They help deal with properties, state, events, and often are responsible for the well-being of other components as well. Keeping track of everything components do sometimes can be tough.

To help with this, React provides us with something known as **lifecycle methods**. Lifecycle methods are (unsurprisingly) special methods that automatically get called as our component goes about its business. They notify us of important milestones in our component's life, and we can use these notifications to simply pay attention or change what our component is about to do.

In this chapter, we look at these lifecycle methods and learn all about what we can do with them.

Meet the Lifecycle Methods

Lifecycle methods are not very complicated. We can think of them as glorified event handlers that get called at various points in a component's life, and just like event handlers, you can write some code to do things at those various points. Before we go further, it is time for you to quickly meet our lifecycle methods. They are:

- `componentWillMount`
- `componentDidMount`
- `componentWillUnmount`
- `componentWillUpdate`
- `componentDidUpdate`
- `shouldComponentUpdate`
- `componentWillReceiveProps`

We aren't quite done yet. There are three more methods that we are going to throw into the mix even though they aren't strictly lifecycle methods, and they are:

- `getInitialState`
- `getDefaultProps`
- `render`

Some of these names probably sound familiar to you, and some you are probably seeing for the first time. Don't worry. By the end of all this, you'll be on a first name basis with all of them! What we are going to do is look at these lifecycle methods from various angles—starting with some code!

See the Lifecycle Methods in Action

Learning about these lifecycle methods is about as exciting as memorizing names for foreign places (or distant star systems!) you have no plans to visit. To help make all of this more bearable, I am going to first have you play with them through a simple example before we get all academic and read about them.

To play with this example, go to the following URL: https://www.kirupa.com/react/lifecycle _example.htm Once this page loads, you'll see a variation of the counter example we saw earlier (see Figure 11-1).

Figure 11-1   A variation on the counter example.

Don't click on the button or anything just yet. If you have already clicked on the button, just refresh the page to start the example from the beginning. There is a reason why I am saying that, and it isn't because my OCD is acting up :P We want to see this page as it is before we interact with it!

Now, bring up your browser's developer tools and take a look at the Console tab. In Chrome, you'll see something that looks like Figure 11-2.

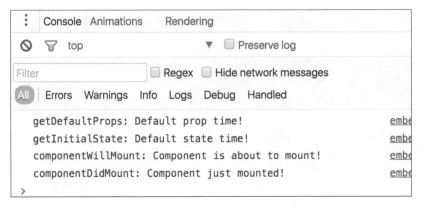

Figure 11-2   The Console view in Chrome.

Notice what you see printed. You will see some messages, and these messages start out with the name of what looks like a lifecycle method. If you click on the plus button once, notice that your Console will show more lifecycle methods getting called (see Figure 11-3).

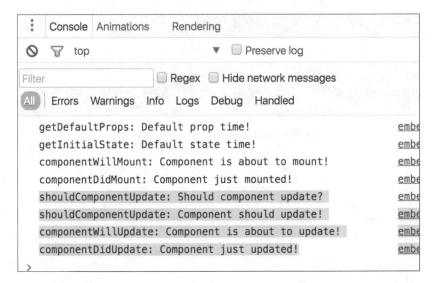

Figure 11-3   More lifecycle methods getting called.

Play with this example for a bit. What this example does is allow you to place all of these lifecycle methods in the context of a component that we've already seen earlier. As you keep hitting the plus button, more lifecycle method entries will show up. Eventually, once your counter approaches a value of 5, your example will just disappear with the following entry showing up in your console: componentWillUnmount: Component is about to be removed from the DOM! At this point, you have reached the end of this example. Of course, to start over, you can just refresh the page!

Now that you've seen the example, let's take a quick look at the component that is responsible for all of this:

```javascript
var CounterParent = React.createClass({
  getDefaultProps: function(){
    console.log("getDefaultProps: Default prop time!");
    return {};
  },
  getInitialState: function() {
    console.log("getInitialState: Default state time!");
    return {
      count: 0
    };
  },
  increase: function() {
    this.setState({
      count: this.state.count + 1
    });
  },
  componentWillUpdate: function(newProps, newState) {
    console.log("componentWillUpdate: Component is about to update!");
  },
  componentDidUpdate: function(currentProps, currentState) {
    console.log("componentDidUpdate: Component just updated!");
  },
  componentWillMount: function() {
    console.log("componentWillMount: Component is about to mount!");
  },
  componentDidMount: function() {
    console.log("componentDidMount: Component just mounted!");
  },
  componentWillUnmount: function() {
    console.log("componentWillUnmount: Component is about to be removed from the
DOM!");
  },
  shouldComponentUpdate: function(newProps, newState) {
    console.log("shouldComponentUpdate: Should component update?");

    if (newState.count < 5) {
      console.log("shouldComponentUpdate: Component should update!");
      return true;
    } else {
      ReactDOM.unmountComponentAtNode(destination);
      console.log("shouldComponentUpdate: Component should not update!");
      return false;
    }
  },
```

```
componentWillReceiveProps: function(newProps){
  console.log("componentWillReceiveProps: Component will get new props!");
},
render: function() {
    var backgroundStyle = {
      padding: 50,
      border: "#333 2px dotted",
      width: 250,
      height: 100,
      borderRadius: 10,
      textAlign: "center"
    };

    return (
      <div style={backgroundStyle}>
        <Counter display={this.state.count}/>
        <button onClick={this.increase}>
          +
        </button>
      </div>
    );
  }
});
```

Take a few moments to look what all of this code does. It seems lengthy, but a bulk of it is just each lifecycle method listed with a `console.log` statement defined. Once you've gone through this code, play with the example one more time. Trust me. *The more time you spend in the example and figure out what is going on, the more fun you are going to have.* The following sections where we look at each lifecycle method across the rendering, updating, and unmounting phases is going to be dreadfully boring. Don't say I didn't warn you.

The Initial Rendering Phase

When your component is about to start its life and make its way to the DOM, the following lifecycle methods get called (see Figure 11-4).

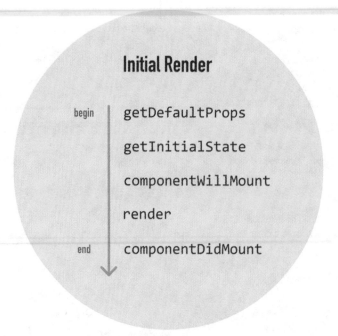

Figure 11-4   The lifecycle methods called initially.

What you saw in your console when the example was loaded was a less colorful version of what you saw here. Now, we are going to go a bit further and learn more about what each of these lifecycle methods do.

getDefaultProps

This method allows you to specify the default value of `this.props`. It gets called before your component is even created or any props from parents are passed in.

getInitialState

This method allows you to specify the default value of `this.state` before your component is created. Just like `getDefaultProps`, it too gets called before your component is created.

componentWillMount

This is the last method that gets called before your component gets rendered to the DOM. There is an important thing to note here. If you were to call `setState` inside this method, your component will not re-render (aka have the `render` method get called and update what gets displayed on screen).

render

This one should be very familiar to you by now. Every component must have this method defined, and it is responsible for returning a single root node (which may have many child nodes inside it). If you don't wish to render anything (for some fancy optimization you might be going for), simply return **null** or **false**.

componentDidMount

This method gets called immediately after your component renders and gets placed on the DOM. At this point, you can safely perform any DOM querying operations without worrying about whether your component has made it or not. If you have any code that depends on your component being ready, you can specify all of that code here as well.

With the exception of the `render` method, all of these lifecycle methods **can fire only once**. That's quite different from the methods we are about to see next.

The Updating Phase

After your components get added to the DOM, they can potentially update and re-render when a prop or state change occurs. During this time, a different collection of lifecycle methods will get called. Yawn. Sorry...

Dealing with State Changes

First, let's look at a state change! When a state change occurs, we mentioned earlier that your component will call its `render` method again. Any components that rely on the output of this component will also get their `render` methods called as well. This is done to ensure that our component is always displaying the latest version of itself. All of that is true, but that is only a partial representation of what happens.

When a state change happens, all the lifecycle methods in Figure 11-5 get called.

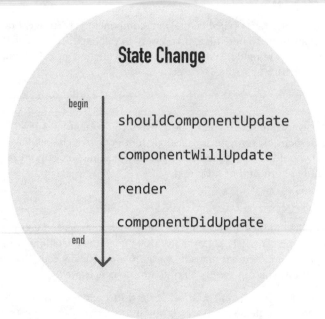

Figure 11-5   Lifecycle methods called when a state change happens.

What these lifecycle methods do is outlined in the following sections.

shouldComponentUpdate

Sometimes, you don't want your component to update when a state change occurs. This method allows you to control this updating behavior. If you use this method and return a **true** value, the component will update. If this method returns a **false** value, this component will skip updating.

That probably sounds a little bit confusing, so here is a simple snippet:

```
shouldComponentUpdate: function(newProps, newState) {

  if (newState.id <= 2) {
    console.log("Component should update!");

    return true;
  } else {
    console.log("Component should not update!");

    return false;
  }
}
```

This method gets called with two arguments which we name `newProps` and `newState`. What we are doing in this snippet of code is checking whether the new value of our `id` state property is less than or equal to 2. If the value is less than or equal to 2, we return **true** to indicate that this component should update. If the value is not less than or equal to 2, we return **false** to indicate that this component should not update.

componentWillUpdate

This method gets called just before your component is about to update. Nothing too exciting here. One thing to note is that you can't change your state by calling `this.setState` from this method.

render

If you didn't override the update via `shouldComponentUpdate` (by returning **false**), the code inside `render` will get called again to ensure your component displays itself properly.

componentDidUpdate

This method gets called after your component updates and the `render` method has been called. If you need to execute any code after the update takes place, this is the place to stash it.

Dealing with Prop Changes

The other time your component updates is when its prop value changes after it has been rendered into the DOM. In this scenario, the lifecycle methods in Figure 11-6 get called.

Figure 11-6   Lifecycle methods when the component's prop value changes.

The only method that is new here is `componentWillReceiveProps`. This method returns one argument, and this argument is an object that contains the new prop values that are about to be assigned to it.

We saw the rest of the lifecycle methods earlier when looking at state changes, so let's not revisit them again. Their behavior is identical when dealing with a prop change.

The Unmounting Phase

The last phase we are going to look at is when your component is about to be destroyed and removed from the DOM (see Figure 11-7).

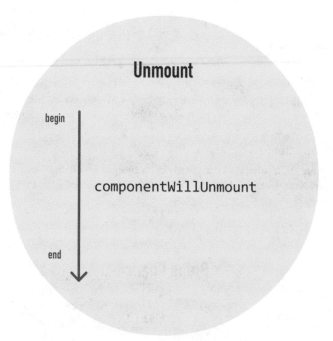

Figure 11-7   Only one lifecycle method is active when your component is about to be destroyed and removed from the DOM.

There is only one lifecycle method that is active here, and that is `componentWillUnmount`. You'll perform any cleanup-related tasks here such as removing event listeners, stopping timers, etc. After this method gets called, your component is removed from the DOM and you can say *Bye!* to it.

Conclusion

Our components are fascinating little things. On the surface they seem like they don't have much going on. Like a good documentary about the oceans, when we look a little deeper and closer, it's almost like seeing a whole other world. As it turns out, React is constantly watching and notifying your component every time something interesting happens. All of this is done via the (extremely boring) lifecycle methods that we spent this entire tutorial looking at. Now, I want to reassure you that knowing what each lifecycle method does and when it gets called will come in handy one day. Everything you've learned isn't just trivial knowledge, though your friends will be impressed if you can describe all of the lifecycle methods from memory. Go ahead and try it the next time you see them.

12

Accessing DOM Elements

There will be times when you want to access properties and methods on an HTML element directly. In our React-colored world where JSX represents everything that is good and pure about markup, why would you ever want to deal directly with the horribleness that is HTML? As you will find out (if you haven't already), there are many cases where dealing with HTML elements through the JavaScript DOM API directly is easier than fiddling with "the React way" of doing things.

To highlight one such situation, take a look at the **Colorizer** example in Figure 12-1.

Figure 12-1 Colorizer example.

If you have access to a browser, you can view it live at the following location: https://www
.kirupa.com/react/examples/colorizer.htm

The **Colorizer** colorizes the (currently) white square with whatever color you provide it. To see
it in action, enter a color value inside the text field and click/tap on the *go* button. If you don't
have any idea of what color to enter, **yellow** is a good one! Once you have provided a color and
submitted it, the white square will turn whatever color value you provided (see Figure 12-2).

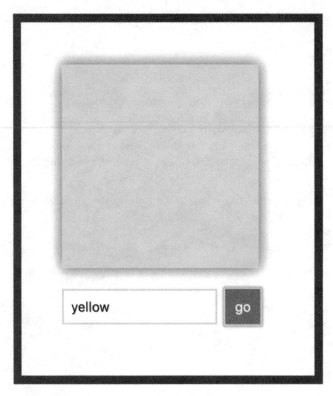

Figure 12-2   The white square turns yellow.

That the square changes color for any valid color value you submit is pretty awesome, but it
isn't what I want you to focus on. Instead, pay attention to the text field and the button after
you submit a value. Notice that the button gets focus, and the color value you just submitted is
still displayed inside the form. If you want to enter another color value, you need to explicitly
return focus to the text field and clear out whatever current value is present. Eww! That seems
unnecessary, and we can do better than that from a usability point of view!

Now, wouldn't it be great if we could clear both the existing color value and return focus to the
text field immediately after you submit a color? That would mean that if we submitted a color
value of **purple**, what we would see afterwards would look like Figure 12-3.

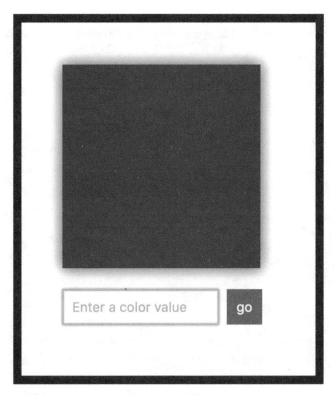

Figure 12-3   We get purple and the text field is ready for the next color.

The entered value of **purple** is cleared, and the focus is returned to the text field. This allows us to enter additional color values and submit them easily without having to manually keep jumping focus back and forth between the text field and the button. Isn't that much nicer?

Getting this behavior right using JSX and traditional React techniques is hard. We aren't even going to bother with explaining how to go about that. Getting this behavior right by dealing with the JavaScript DOM API on various HTML elements directly is pretty easy. Guess what we are going to do? In the following sections, we use something known as refs that React provides to help us access the DOM API on HTML elements. This chapter sounds really REALLY boring, but it is going to be a fun one—I'm mostly sure of it.

Meet Refs

As you know very well by now, inside our various `render` methods, we've been writing HTML-like things known as JSX. Our JSX is simply a description of what the DOM should look like. It doesn't represent actual HTML—despite looking a whole lot like it. Anyway, to provide a bridge between JSX and the final HTML elements in the DOM, React provides us with something funnily known as **refs** (short for *references*).

The way refs work is a little odd. The easiest way to make sense of it is to look at an example. Let's say we have a `render` method from our **Colorizer** example that looks as follows:

```
render: function() {
  var squareStyle = {
    backgroundColor: this.state.bgColor
  };

  return (
    <div className="colorArea">
      <div style={squareStyle} className="colorSquare"></div>

      <form onSubmit={this.setNewColor}>
        <input
          onChange={this.colorValue}
          placeholder="Enter a color value">
        </input>
        <button type="submit">go</button>
      </form>
    </div>
  );
}
```

Inside this `render` method, we are returning a big chunk of JSX representing (among other things) the `input` element where we enter our color value. What we want to do is access the `input` element's DOM representation so that we can call some APIs on it using JavaScript.

The way we do that using refs is by setting the `ref` attribute on the element we would like to reference the HTML of:

```
render: function() {
  var squareStyle = {
    backgroundColor: this.state.bgColor
  };

  return (
    <div className="colorArea">
      <div style={squareStyle} className="colorSquare"></div>

      <form onSubmit={this.setNewColor}>
        <input
          ref={}
          onChange={this.colorValue}
          placeholder="Enter a color value">
        </input>
        <button type="submit">go</button>
      </form>
    </div>
  );
}
```

Because we are interested in the `input` element, our `ref` attribute is attached to it. Right now, our `ref` attribute is empty. What you typically set as the `ref` attribute's value is a JavaScript callback function. This function gets called automatically when the component housing this render method gets mounted. If we set our `ref` attribute's value to a simple JavaScript function that stores a reference to the referenced DOM element, it would look something like the following highlighted lines:

```
 1  render: function() {
 2    var squareStyle = {
 3      backgroundColor: this.state.bgColor
 4    };
 5
 6    var self = this;
 7
 8    return (
 9      <div className="colorArea">
10        <div style={squareStyle} className="colorSquare"></div>
11
12        <form onSubmit={this.setNewColor}>
13          <input
14            ref={
15                    function(el) {
16                      self._input = el;
17                    }
18                  }
19            onChange={this.colorValue}
20            placeholder="Enter a color value">
21          </input>
22          <button type="submit">go</button>
23        </form>
24      </div>
25    );
26  }
```

The end result of this code running once our component mounts is simple: we can access the HTML representing our `input` element from anywhere inside our component by calling `this._input`. Take a few moments to see how the highlighted lines of code help do that. Once you are done, we'll walk through this code together.

First, our callback function looks as follows:

```
function(el) {
    self._input = el;
}
```

This anonymous function gets called when our component mounts, and a reference to the final HTML DOM element is passed in as an argument. We capture this argument using the `el` identifier, but you can use any name for this argument that you want. The body of this callback function simply sets a custom property called `_input` to the value of our DOM element. To ensure we create this property on our component, we use the `self` variable to create a closure where the `this` in question refers to our component as opposed to the callback function itself. (Autobinding doesn't happen automatically this time around!)

Taking a step back and looking at the bigger picture that ties everything together including the `render` method we just saw, let's look at the full `Colorizer` component with all of the `ref`-related shenanigans highlighted:

```
var Colorizer = React.createClass({
    getInitialState: function() {
      return {
          color: '',
          bgColor: ''
      }
    },
    colorValue: function(e) {
      this.setState({color: e.target.value});
    },
    setNewColor: function(e){
      this.setState({bgColor: this.state.color});

      this._input.value = "";
      this._input.focus();

      e.preventDefault();
    },
    render: function() {
      var squareStyle = {
        backgroundColor: this.state.bgColor
      };

      var self = this;

      return (
        <div className="colorArea">
          <div style={squareStyle} className="colorSquare"></div>

          <form onSubmit={this.setNewColor}>
            <input
                ref={
                      function(el) {
                        self._input = el;
                      }
                    }
                onChange={this.colorValue}
                placeholder="Enter a color value">
            </input>
            <button type="submit">go</button>
          </form>
        </div>
      );
    }
});
```

Focusing just on what happens to our `input` element, when the form gets submitted and the `setNewColor` method gets called, we clear the contents of our `input` element by calling `this._input.value = ""`. We set focus to our `input` element by calling `this._input.focus()`. All of our `ref-` related work was simply to enable these two lines where we needed some way to have `this._input` point to the HTML element representing our `input` element that we define in JSX. Once we figured that out, we just call the `value` property and `focus` method the DOM API exposes on this element.

Simplifying Further with ES6 Arrow Functions

Learning React is hard enough, so I have tried to shy away from forcing you to use ES6 techniques by default. When it comes to working with the `ref` attribute, using arrow functions to deal with the callback function does simplify matters a bit. This is one of those cases where I recommend you use an ES6 technique.

As you saw a few moments ago, to assign a property on our component to the referenced HTML element, we did something like this:

```
<input
    ref={
            function(el) {
              self._input = el;
            }
        }
    onChange={this.colorValue}
    placeholder="Enter a color value">
</input>
```

To deal with scoping shenanigans, we created a `self` variable initialized to `this` to ensure we created the `_input` property on our component. That seems unnecessarily messy.

Using arrow functions, we can simplify all of this down to just the following:

```
<input
    ref={
            (el) => this._input = el
        }
    onChange={this.colorValue}
    placeholder="Enter a color value">
</input>
```

The end result is identical to what we spent all of this time looking at, and because of how arrow functions deal with scope, you can use `this` inside the function body and reference the component without doing any extra work. No need for an outer `self` variable equivalent!

Conclusion

In this tutorial, we saw how "easy" it is to access a DOM element directly. React used to provide a much easier way of referencing elements. You could set the `refs` attribute on an element and initialize it to a string value:

```
<button refs="myButton">Click me!</button>
```

You could then access this element after the component was mounted by doing something like `this.refs.myButton`. Before you get really excited about using something like this over our function callback approach with the `ref` attribute, this string-based approach is likely to be deprecated. It works at the moment of this writing, but who knows when it will stop working. Now, given that this is going away, you may be wondering why I told you about this. To be frank, I really have no idea :P

13

Creating a Single-Page App
Using React Router

Now that you've familiarized yourself with the basics of how to work with React, let's kick
things up a few notches. What we are going to do is use React to build a simple, **single-page
app** (also referred to as **SPA** by the cool kids—and people living in Scandinavia). As we talked
about in Chapter 1 forever ago, single-page apps are different from the more traditional
multi-page apps that you see everywhere. The biggest difference is that navigating a single-page
app doesn't involve going to an entirely new page. Instead, your pages (commonly known
as **views** in this context) typically load inline within the same page as illustrated in Figure 13-1.

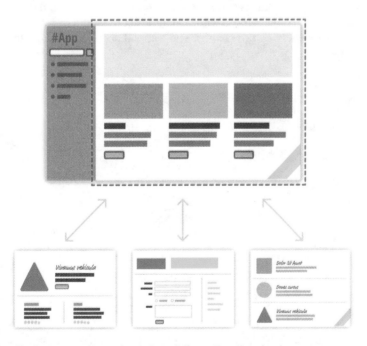

Figure 13-1   Single-page apps use load views inline rather than load new pages.

When you are loading content inline, things get a little challenging. The hard part is not loading the content itself. That is relatively easy. The hard part is making sure that single-page apps behave in a way that is consistent with what your users are used to. More specifically, when users navigate your app, they expect that:

1. The URL displayed in the address bar always reflects the thing that they are viewing.

2. They can use the browser's back and forward buttons—successfully.

3. They can navigate to a particular view (aka **deep link**) directly using the appropriate URL.

With multi-page apps, these three things come for free. There is nothing extra you have to do for any of it. With single-page apps, because you aren't navigating to an entirely new page, you have to do real work to deal with these three things *that your users expect to just work*. You need to ensure that navigating within your app adjusts the URL appropriately. You need to ensure your browser's history is properly synchronized with each navigation to allow users to use the back and forward buttons. If users bookmark a particular view or copy/paste a URL to access later, you need to ensure that your single-page app takes the user to the correct place.

To deal with all of this, you have a bucket full of techniques commonly known as **routing**. Routing is where you try to map URLs to destinations that aren't physical pages, such as the individual views in your single-page app. That sounds complicated, but fortunately there are a bunch of JavaScript libraries that help us out with this. One such JavaScript library is the star of this chapter, React Router (https://github.com/reactjs/react-router). React Router provides routing capabilities to single-page apps built in React, and what makes it nice is that it extends what you already know about React in familiar ways to give you all of this routing awesomeness. In this chapter, you learn all about how it does that—and hopefully more!

The Example

Before we go further, let's take a look at an example (see Figure 13-2).

Figure 13-2   A simple React app that uses React Router.

What you have here is a simple React app that uses React Router to provide all of the navigation and view-loading goodness! While the screenshot of the app looks nice and all, this is one of those cases where you want to play with the app to see more of what it does. Go ahead and open this page (https://www.kirupa.com/react/examples/react_router_final.htm) in its own browser window, click on the various navigation tabs to see the different views, and use the back and forward buttons to see them working.

In the following sections, we are going to be building this app in pieces. By the end, not only will you have recreated this app, you'll hopefully have learned enough about React Router to build cooler and more awesomer things.

Building the App

The first thing we need to do is get the boilerplate markup and code for our app up and running. Create a new HTML document and add the following content into it:

```
<!DOCTYPE html>
<html>

<head>
  <title>React! React! React!</title>
  <script src="https://unpkg.com/react@15.3.2/dist/react.js"></script>
  <script src="https://unpkg.com/react-dom@15.3.2/dist/react-dom.js"></script>
  <script src="https://cdnjs.cloudflare.com/ajax/libs/babel-core/5.8.23/browser.min
.js"></script>

  <style>

  </style>
</head>

<body>

  <div id="container">

  </div>

  <script type="text/babel">
    var destination = document.querySelector("#container");

    ReactDOM.render(
      <div>
        Hello!
      </div>,
      destination
    );
  </script>
</body>

</html>
```

This starting point is almost the same as what you've seen for all of our other examples. This is just a nearly blank app that happens to load the React and React-DOM libraries. If you preview what you have in your browser, you'll see a very lonely **Hello!** displayed.

> ### Note: Still Keeping Things Simple
>
> For now, we are continuing to rely on having our browser do all of the heavy lifting. We'll look into changing that up with a "modern" build process later, so enjoy the simplicity for now :P

Next, because React Router isn't a part of React itself, we need to add a reference to it. In our markup, find where we have our existing script references and add the following highlighted line:

```
<script src="https://unpkg.com/react@15.3.2/dist/react.js"></script>
<script src="https://unpkg.com/react-dom@15.3.2/dist/react-dom.js"></script>
<script src="https://cdnjs.cloudflare.com/ajax/libs/babel-core/5.8.23/browser.min
.js"></script>
<script src="https://npmcdn.com/react-router/umd/ReactRouter.min.js"></script>
```

By adding the highlighted line, we ensure the React Router library is loaded alongside the core React, ReactDOM, and Babel libraries. At this point, we are in a good state to start building our app and taking advantage of the sweet functionality React Router brings to the table.

Displaying the Initial Frame

When building a single-page app, there will always be a part of your page that will remain static. This static part, also referred to as an **app frame**, could just be one invisible HTML element that acts as the container for all of your content, or it could include some additional visual things like a header, footer, navigation, etc. In our case, our app frame will involve our navigation header and an empty area for content to load in. To display this, we are going to create a component that is going to be responsible for this.

Inside your `script` tag just above your `ReactDOM.render` call, go ahead and add the following chunk of JSX and JavaScript:

```
var App = React.createClass({
  render: function() {
    return (
      <div>
        <h1>Simple SPA</h1>
        <ul className="header">
          <li>Home</li>
          <li>Stuff</li>
          <li>Contact</li>
        </ul>
        <div className="content">

        </div>
      </div>
    )
  }
});
```

Once you have pasted this, take a look at what we have here. What we have is a component called App that returns some HTML. To see what this HTML looks like, modify your ReactDOM. render call to reference this component instead of displaying the word *Hello!* Go ahead and make the following highlighted change:

```
ReactDOM.render(
  <div>
    <App/>
  </div>,
  destination
);
```

Once you have done this, preview your app in the browser. You should see an unstyled version of an app title and some list items (see Figure 13-3).

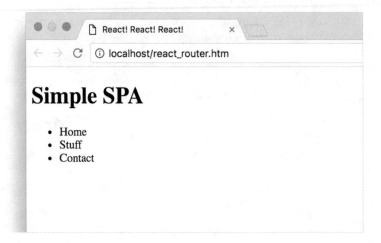

Figure 13-3   Unstyled version.

I know that this doesn't look all fancy and styled, but that's OK for now. We will deal with that later. Going a bit deeper, what we've done is just create a component called App and display it via our ReactDOM.render call. The important thing to call out is that there is nothing React Router - specific here. ABSOLUTELY NOTHING! This is straight-up React 101. Let's fix that by throwing React Router into the mix. Replace the contents of your ReactDOM.render call with the following:

```
ReactDOM.render(
  <ReactRouter.Router>
    <ReactRouter.Route path="/" component={App}>

    </ReactRouter.Route>
  </ReactRouter.Router>,
  destination
);
```

Ignore how strange everything looks for a moment, and just preview your app in the browser after you've made this change. If everything worked out properly, you will see your App component displayed just like you saw earlier. Now, let's figure out why that is the case by learning more about what exactly is going on here. This is where we deviate a bit from core React concepts and learn things specific to React Router itself.

First, what we did is specify our `Router` component:

```
ReactDOM.render(
  <ReactRouter.Router>
    <ReactRouter.Route path="/" component={App}>

    </ReactRouter.Route>
  </ReactRouter.Router>,
  destination
);
```

The `Router` component is part of the React Router API, and its job is to deal with all of the routing-related logic our app will need. Inside this component, we specify what is known as the **routing configuration**. That is a fancy term that people use to describe the mapping between URLs and the views. The specifics of that are handled by another component called `Route`:

```
ReactDOM.render(
  <ReactRouter.Router>
    <ReactRouter.Route path="/" component={App}>

    </ReactRouter.Route>
  </ReactRouter.Router>,
  destination
);
```

The `Route` component takes several props that help define what to display at what URL. The `path` prop specifies the URL we are interested in matching. In this case, it is the root, aka /. The `component` prop allows you to specify the name of the component you wish to display. For this example, it is our App component. Putting this all together, what this Route says is as follows: *If the URL you are on contains the root, go ahead and display the App component.* Because this condition is true when you preview your app, you see the result of what happens when your App component renders.

Displaying the Home Page

As you can sorta kinda see, the way React Router provides you with all of this routing functionality is by using concepts in React you are already familiar with—namely **components**, **props**, and **JSX**. What we have right now for displaying our app's frame is a great example of this. Now, it's time to go even further. What we want to do next is define the content that we will display as part of our home view.

To do this, we are going to create a component called **Home** that is going to contain the markup we want to display. Just above where you have your App component defined, add the following:

```
var Home = React.createClass({
  render: function() {
      return (
        <div>
          <h2>HELLO</h2>
          <p>Cras facilisis urna ornare ex volutpat, et
          convallis erat elementum. Ut aliquam, ipsum vitae
          gravida suscipit, metus dui bibendum est, eget rhoncus nibh
          metus nec massa. Maecenas hendrerit laoreet augue
          nec molestie. Cum sociis natoque penatibus et magnis
          dis parturient montes, nascetur ridiculus mus.</p>

          <p>Duis a turpis sed lacus dapibus elementum sed eu lectus.</p>
        </div>
      );
    }
});
```

As you can see, our Home component doesn't do anything special. It just returns a blob of HTML. Now, what we want to do is display the contents of our Home component when the page loads. This component is the equivalent of our app's "home page." The way we do this is simple. Inside our App component, we have a div with a class value of **content**. We are going to load our Home component inside there.

The obvious solution might look something like this:

```
var App = React.createClass({
  render: function() {
    return (
      <div>
        <h1>Simple SPA</h1>
        <ul className="header">
          <li>Home</li>
          <li>Stuff</li>
          <li>Contact</li>
        </ul>
        <div className="content">
          <Home/>
        </div>
      </div>
    )
  }
});
```

Notice that we define our `Home` component inside that content `div`. If you preview your app, things will even seem to work as expected (see Figure 13-4).

Figure 13-4   Increased functionality.

You see your navigation header, and then you see the contents of our `Home` component. While this approach works, it is actually the wrong thing to do. It is wrong because it complicates our desire to load other pieces of content as the user is navigating around our app. We've essentially hard-coded our app to only display the `Home` component. That's a problem, but we'll come back to that in a little bit.

Interim Cleanup Time

Before we continue making progress on our app, let's take a short break and make some stylistic improvements to what we have so far.

Adding the CSS

Right now, our app looks very plain...and like something straight out of the 1800s. To fix this, we are going to rely on our dear old friend, CSS. Inside the `style` tag, go ahead and add the following style rules:

```
body {
  background-color: #FFCC00;
  padding: 20px;
  margin: 0;
}
```

```css
h1, h2, p, ul, li {
  font-family: Helvetica, Arial, sans-serif;
}
ul.header li {
  display: inline;
  list-style-type: none;
  margin: 0;
}
ul.header {
  background-color: #111;
  padding: 0;
}
ul.header li a {
  color: #FFF;
  font-weight: bold;
  text-decoration: none;
  padding: 20px;
  display: inline-block;
}
.content {
  background-color: #FFF;
  padding: 20px;
}
.content h2 {
  padding: 0;
  margin: 0;
}
.content li {
  margin-bottom: 10px;
}
```

Yes, we are using CSS in its markup form. We aren't doing the inline style object approach that we saw in Chapter 4. The reason has to do with convenience. Our components aren't going to be re-used outside of our particular app, and we really want to take advantage of CSS inheritance to minimize duplicated markup. Otherwise, if we didn't use regular CSS, we'll end up with a bunch of giant style objects defined for almost every element in our markup. That would make even the most patient among us annoyed when reading the code.

Anyway, once you have added all of this CSS, our app will start to look much better (see Figure 13-5).

Figure 13-5   CSS styling added.

There is still some more work to be done (for example, our navigation links disappeared behind the black banner), but we'll fix all of those up in a little bit.

Avoiding the ReactRouter Prefix

We have just one more cleanup related task before we return to our regularly scheduled programming. Have you noticed that every single time we call something defined by the React Router API, we prefix that something with the word `ReactRouter`?

```
<ReactRouter.Router>
  <ReactRouter.Route path="/" component={App}>

  </ReactRouter.Route>
</ReactRouter.Router>
```

That is a bit verbose to have to repeat for every API call we make, and this is going to be more of a problem as we dive further into the React Router API and use more things from inside it.

The fix for this involves using a new ES6 trick where you can manually specify which values will automatically get prefixed. Towards the top of your `script` tag, add the following:

```
var { Router,
      Route,
      IndexRoute,
      IndexLink,
      Link } = ReactRouter;
```

Once you've added this code, every time you use one of the values defined inside the brackets, the prefix **ReactRouter** will automatically be added for you when your app runs. This means, you can now go back to your `ReactDOM.render` method and remove the **ReactRouter** prefix from our `Router` and `Route` component instances:

```
ReactDOM.render(
  <Router>
    <Route path="/" component={App}>

    </Route>
  </Router>,
  destination
);
```

If you preview your app now, nothing really should change. The end result is identical to what you had before. The only difference is that our markup is a bit more compact.

Now, before we move on, you are probably wondering why the list of values that will automatically be prefixed with **ReactRouter** contains a whole bunch of things beyond the **Router** and **Route** values that we have used in our code so far. Think of these additional values as a preview of the other parts of the React Router API we will be using shortly. Spoiler alert! (Probably too late to mention that now, eh?)

Displaying the Home Page Correctly

We ended a few sections ago by saying that the way we currently have our home page displayed is incorrect. Although you get the desired result when our page loads, this approach doesn't really make it easy for us to load anything other than the home page when users navigate around. The call to our `Home` component is hard-coded inside `App`.

The correct solution involves letting React Router handle which component to call depending on what your current URL structure is. This involves nesting `Route` components inside `Route` components to better define the URL-to-view mapping. Go back to our `ReactDOM.render` method, and make the following highlighted change:

```
ReactDOM.render(
  <Router>
    <Route path="/" component={App}>
      <IndexRoute component={Home}/>
    </Route>
  </Router>,
  destination
);
```

Inside our root `Route` element, we are defining another `Route` element of type `IndexRoute` (more on who this is in a second!) and setting its view to be our `Home` component. There is one more change we need to make. Inside our `App` component, remove the call to the `Home` component and replace it with the following highlighted line:

```
var App = React.createClass({
  render: function() {
    return (
      <div>
        <h1>Simple SPA</h1>
        <ul className="header">
          <li>Home</li>
          <li>Stuff</li>
          <li>Contact</li>
        </ul>
        <div className="content">
          {this.props.children}
        </div>
      </div>
    )
  }
});
```

If you preview your page now, you will still see your Home content displayed. The difference this time is that we are displaying the Home content properly in a way that doesn't prevent other content from being displayed instead. This is because of two things:

1. What gets displayed inside `App` is controlled by the result of `this.props.children` instead of a hard-coded component.

2. Our `Route` element inside `ReactDOM.render` contains an `IndexRoute` element whose sole purpose for existing is to declare which component will be displayed when your app initially loads.

All of this may seem even more bizarre than what you expected a few moments ago, but things will make more sense as we use these various APIs more in the following sections.

Creating the Navigation Links

Right now, we just have our frame and home view setup. There isn't really anything else for a user to do here outside of just seeing what we have set as the home page. Let's fix that by creating some navigation links. More specifically, let's linkify the navigation elements we already have:

```
var App = React.createClass({
  render: function() {
    return (
      <div>
        <h1>Simple SPA</h1>
        <ul className="header">
          <li>Home</li>
          <li>Stuff</li>
          <li>Contact</li>
```

```
      </ul>
      <div className="content">
        {this.props.children}
      </div>
    </div>
    )
  }
});
```

If you aren't sure why these elements aren't visible when you preview your page, that's because they blended in with the black background once we added the CSS in. No biggie there. We'll fix that in a few, but first let's talk about how we are going to turn these elements into links.

The way you specify navigation links in React Router isn't by *directly* using the tried and tested a tag and throwing in a path via the href attribute. Instead, you specify your navigation link using React Router's Link components that are similar to a tags but offer a lot more functionality. To see the Link component in action, go ahead and modify our existing navigation elements to look like the following highlighted lines:

```
var App = React.createClass({
  render: function() {
    return (
      <div>
        <h1>Simple SPA</h1>
        <ul className="header">
          <li><Link to="/">Home</Link></li>
          <li><Link to="/stuff">Stuff</Link></li>
          <li><Link to="/contact">Contact</Link></li>
        </ul>
        <div className="content">
          {this.props.children}
        </div>
      </div>
    )
  }
});
```

Notice what have done here. Our Link components specify a prop called to. This prop **specifies the value of the URL we will display in the address bar**. Indirectly, it also specifies the location we will be telling React Router we are virtually navigating to. Our Home link takes users to the root (/), the Stuff link takes users to a location called **stuff**, and the Contact link takes users to a location called **contact**.

If you preview your page and click on the links (which will now be visible because the CSS for them will have kicked in), you won't see anything new display. You will just see your Home content because that is all that we had specified earlier. With that said, you can see the URLs updating in the address bar. You'll see your current page followed by a #/**contact**, #/**stuff**, or #/ depending on which of the links you clicked. Oh, you'll also see a random hash added after the URL. That is progress!

Adding the Stuff and Contact Views

Our app is slowly taking its final shape...or it will get really close by the time we are done with this section! What we are going to do next is define the components for our Stuff and Contact views that we linked to earlier. In your code just below where you have your Home component, go ahead and add in the following:

```
var Contact = React.createClass({
  render: function() {
      return (
        <div>
          <h2>GOT QUESTIONS?</h2>
          <p>The easiest thing to do is post on
          our <a href="http://forum.kirupa.com">forums</a>.
          </p>
        </div>
      );
    }
});


var Stuff = React.createClass({
  render: function() {
      return (
        <div>
          <h2>STUFF</h2>
          <p>Mauris sem velit, vehicula eget sodales vitae,
          rhoncus eget sapien:</p>
          <ol>
            <li>Nulla pulvinar diam</li>
            <li>Facilisis bibendum</li>
            <li>Vestibulum vulputate</li>
            <li>Eget erat</li>
            <li>Id porttitor</li>
          </ol>
        </div>
      );
    }
});
```

What we have just added are the Stuff and Contact components that simply render out HTML. All that remains is for us to update our routing configuration to include these two components and display them at the appropriate URL.

In our ReactDOM.render method, go ahead and add the following two highlighted lines:

```
ReactDOM.render(
  <Router>
    <Route path="/" component={App}>
      <IndexRoute component={Home}/>
```

```
      <Route path="stuff" component={Stuff} />
      <Route path="contact" component={Contact} />
    </Route>
  </Router>,
  destination
);
```

All we are doing here is updating our routing logic to display the Stuff component if the URL contains the word **stuff** and to display the Contact component if the URL contains the word **contact**. If you preview your page now, click on the Stuff and Contact links. If everything worked out fine, you'll see these views get loaded inside our app frame when you navigate to them.

Note: A Little Bit About Route Matching

Our route configuration is nothing more than a series of rules that determine what to do when a URL matches the conditions we have laid out. The fancy term for that is **route matching**. The heuristic React Router uses to match URLs is fully explained in the React Router documentation, but for our case, we have a simple nested route where you can have multiple things that can match at the same time. Our outer route matches if the URL contains /. Our inner routes then match if the URL happens to contain **stuff** or **contact**.

What this means is simple. For each route that matches, the component that you specified to display will appear. When you are navigating to a page like /**stuff**, the App component will display because the / exists in the URL. The Stuff component then displays because the path for **stuff** is in the URL as well. That is why when we navigate to the Stuff or Contact pages, we see them in addition to our frame. You can have deeply nested routes as well.

Take a look at the following configuration:

```
ReactDOM.render(

  <Router>

    <Route path="/" component={App}>

      <IndexRoute component={Home} />

      <Route path="stuff" component={Stuff}>

        <Route path="blah" component={MyBlah}/>

      </Route>

      <Route path="contact" component={Contact} />

    </Route>

  </Router>,

  destination);
```

In this example, notice that our Route element whose path is **stuff** now contains a nested route for a path containing **blah**. This means if you happened to have a URL that is /**stuff/ blah**, the MyBlah component will be displayed in addition to the Stuff component and the App component from the parent routes matching.

By nesting routes and following the route matching rules (https://github.com/reactjs/ react-router/blob/master/docs/guides/RouteMatching.md), you can display custom views depending on a variety of URL arrangements you may expose in your app for your users to navigate to.

Creating Active Links

The last thing we are going to tackle is something that greatly increases the usability of our app. Depending on which page you are currently displaying, we are going to highlight that link with a blue background. For example, Figure 13-6 is what our app will look like when the Stuff content is being displayed.

Figure 13-6   The Stuff content.

The way you accomplish this in React Router is by setting a prop called `activeClassName` on your `Link` instances with the name of the CSS class that will get set when that link is currently active. To make this happen, go back to your `App` component and make the highlighted changes:

```
var App = React.createClass({
  render: function() {
    return (
      <div>
        <h1>Simple SPA</h1>
        <ul className="header">
          <li><Link to="/" activeClassName="active">Home</Link></li>
          <li><Link to="/stuff" activeClassName="active">Stuff</Link></li>
          <li><Link to="/contact" activeClassName="active">Contact</Link></li>
```

```
        </ul>
        <div className="content">
          {this.props.children}
        </div>
      </div>
    )
  }
});
```

We specify the `activeClassName` prop and set it to a value of **active**. This ensures that whenever a link is clicked (and its path becomes active), the link element's `class` attribute at runtime gets set to a value of **active**. To ensure our active links are styled differently, go ahead and add the following CSS:

```
.active {
  background-color: #0099FF;
}
```

If you preview your app now, click on any of the links. Notice that the active link (and the Home link) displays with a blue background. We aren't done just yet, though. Our Home link is always highlighted. It should only be highlighted when we load our Home page for the first time or explicitly navigate to the Home link itself. To fix this, we need to change how we link to our Home content. Instead of specifying our Home content with a `Link` element, we are going to replace it with an `IndexLink` element instead.

Go ahead and make this change:

```
var App = React.createClass({
  render: function() {
    return (
      <div>
        <h1>Simple SPA</h1>
        <ul className="header">
          <li><IndexLink to="/" activeClassName="active">Home</IndexLink></li>
          <li><Link to="/stuff" activeClassName="active">Stuff</Link></li>
          <li><Link to="/contact" activeClassName="active">Contact</Link></li>
        </ul>
        <div className="content">
          {this.props.children}
        </div>
      </div>
    )
  }
});
```

Once your Home navigation element is represented by an `IndexLink` instead of a `Link`, preview your app again. This time, when the app loads, you'll notice that your Home link has the cool blue background by default. When you navigate to the Stuff or Contact pages, the Home link no longer has the highlight applied. And with this, your app is mostly good to go!

Conclusion

By now, we've covered a good chunk of the cool functionality React Router has for helping you build your single-page apps. This doesn't mean that there aren't more interesting things for you to take advantage of. Our app was pretty simple with very modest demands on what routing functionality we needed to implement. There is a whole lot more that React Router provides, so if you are building a more complex single-page app than what we've looked at so far, you should totally spend an afternoon taking a look the full React Router documentation (https://github.com/reactjs/react-router/) and examples.

14

Building a Todo List App

If creating the **Hello, World!** example was a celebration of you getting your feet wet with React, creating the quintessential Todo List app is a celebration of you approaching React mastery! In this chapter, we tie together a lot of the concepts and techniques you've learned to create something that works as follows: https://www.kirupa.com/react/examples/todo.htm

You start off with a blank app that allows you to enter tasks for later (see Figure 14-1).

Figure 14-1   A blank app with task entry.

The way this Todo List app works is pretty simple. Type in a task or whatever you want into the text field and press Add (or hit Enter/Return). Once you've submitted your task, you will see it appear as an entry. You can keep adding tasks to add additional entries and have them all show up (see Figure 14-2).

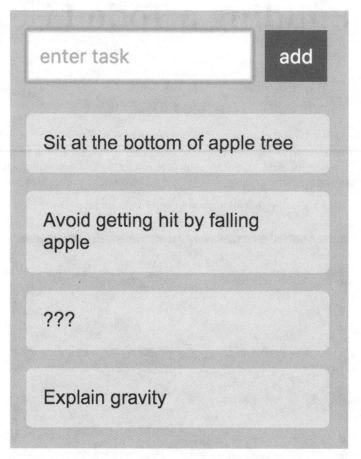

Figure 14-2 You can add tasks and have them show up.

Pretty simple, right? In the following sections, we build this app from scratch and learn (in awesomely painstaking detail) how things work along the way.

Getting Started

By now, you know the drill. We need a starting point, so go ahead and create a new HTML document. Inside it, add the following content into it:

```
<!DOCTYPE html>
<html>

<head>
  <title>React! React! React!</title>
  <script src="https://unpkg.com/react@15.3.2/dist/react.js"></script>
  <script src="https://unpkg.com/react-dom@15.3.2/dist/react-dom.js"></script>
  <script src="https://cdnjs.cloudflare.com/ajax/libs/babel-core/5.8.23/browser.min
.js"></script>

  <style>

  </style>
</head>

<body>

  <div id="container">

  </div>

  <script type="text/babel">
    var destination = document.querySelector("#container");

    ReactDOM.render(
      <div>
        Hello!
      </div>,
      destination
    );
  </script>
</body>

</html>
```

If you preview all of this in the browser, you will see the word **Hello!** appear. If you see that, then you are in good shape. It's time to start building our Todo List app!

Creating the UI

Right now, our app doesn't do a whole lot. We'll fix that by first getting the various UI elements up and running. That isn't very complicated for our app! The first thing we are going to do to is get our input field and button to appear. This is all done by using the div, form, input, and button elements!

All of that will live inside a component we are going to call `TodoList`. Go ahead and add the following code above where you have your `ReactDOM.render` method:

```
var TodoList = React.createClass({
  render: function() {
      return (
        <div className="todoListMain">
          <div className="header">
            <form>
              <input placeholder="enter task">
              </input>
              <button type="submit">add</button>
            </form>
          </div>
        </div>
      );
    }
});
```

Inside your `ReactDOM.render` method, we need to call our newly added `TodoList` component to render it. Go ahead and replace your existing JSX with the following:

```
ReactDOM.render(
  <div>
    <TodoList/>
  </div>,
  destination
);
```

Save your changes and preview what you have right now in your browser. You'll see something that looks like Figure 14-3.

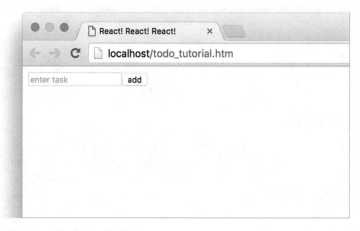

Figure 14-3   What you should see in the browser.

If you are surprised at what you see, take a few moments to look at the JSX we defined inside the `TodoList` component. There shouldn't be anything surprising there. We just defined a handful of HTML elements that look really REALLY boring. Speaking of that, let's make our HTML elements look less boring by introducing them to so some CSS!

Inside your `style` block, add the following:

```css
body {
  padding: 50px;
  background-color: #66CCFF;
  font-family: sans-serif;
}
.todoListMain .header input {
  padding: 10px;
  font-size: 16px;
  border: 2px solid #FFF;
}
.todoListMain .header button {
  padding: 10px;
  font-size: 16px;
  margin: 10px;
  background-color: #0066FF;
  color: #FFF;
  border: 2px solid #0066FF;
}

.todoListMain .header button:hover {
  background-color: #003399;
  border: 2px solid #003399;
  cursor: pointer;
}
```

Once you've added all of this, preview your app now. Because our HTML elements had the appropriate `className` values set on them, our CSS will kick in and our example will now look like Figure 14-4.

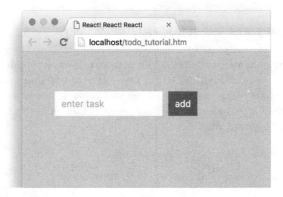

Figure 14-4   The improved example.

At this point, our app looks pretty good. It doesn't do much, but at least we are making progress. In the next section, we will start to make our app actually do things.

Creating the Functionality

The actual implementation of our Todo List app functionality is not as crazy as you might think. Let's take a high-level view of how it works. The most important piece of data is the text you enter into the text field. Each time you enter some text and submit the form, that text gets visually displayed in a list below any previous pieces of text you submitted. So far, this makes sense, right?

All of this is done by simply taking advantage of React's state functionality. Inside our `state` object, we have an array that is responsible for storing everything you enter (see Figure 14-5).

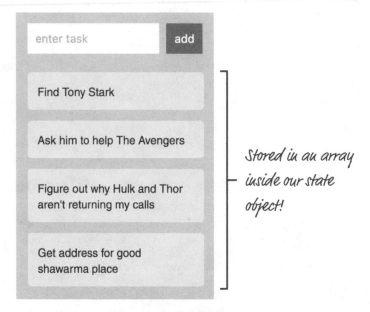

Figure 14-5   Our tasks are stored in an array. I know. Not very exciting :-(

Each time this array of items gets updated with new text that you submit, we update what you see with the newly submitted text. The rest of the work is just around setting up events and event handlers to ensure we can submit the form and know exactly what text to add to our array of items. In the following sections, we are going to turn all of this English we've seen here into React-flavored JavaScript and JSX!

Initializing our State Object

The first thing we are going to do is initialize our state object with the array that will be responsible for storing all of the submitted text. Inside our `TodoList` component, add the following highlighted lines:

```
var TodoList = React.createClass({
  getInitialState: function() {
    return {
      items: []
    };
  },
  render: function() {
    return (
        <div className="todoListMain">
          <div className="header">
            <form>
              <input placeholder="enter task">
              </input>
              <button type="submit">add</button>
            </form>
          </div>
        </div>
    );
  }
});
```

What we are doing here is specifying the `getInitialState` method that gets called before our component renders. Inside that method, we create an empty array called `items` that we can then access via `this.state.items` from anywhere inside this component.

Handling the Form Submit

We add new items to our todo list when you submit the form either by pressing the Add button or hitting Enter/Return on your keyboard. This behavior is mostly builtin to HTML and our browsers know all about how to deal with this. We don't have to write any special code for dealing with the Enter/Return key or listening for a press on the Add button. The only thing we need to worry about is dealing with what happens when the form actually gets submitted.

To do that, we listen to the **onSubmit** event on our `form` element. This event is fired every time the form is submitted, and that includes hitting the Enter/Return key or fiddling with any element that has a `type` attribute of **submit** on it. When the form is submitted and that event gets overheard, we will need to call an event handler. Let's give that event handler a name of `addItem`.

Putting all of this together, inside your `TodoList` component's `render` function, make the following highlighted change:

```
render: function() {
  return (
    <div className="todoListMain">
      <div className="header">
        <form onSubmit={this.addItem}>
          <input placeholder="enter task">
          </input>
          <button type="submit">add</button>
        </form>
      </div>
    </div>
  );
}
```

As we had hoped to do, we just linked our `form` element's **onSubmit** event to the `addItem` event handler. This event handler doesn't exist, but we are going to fix that by adding the following highlighted lines:

```
var TodoList = React.createClass({
  getInitialState: function() {
    return {
      items: []
    };
  },
  addItem: function(e) {

  },
  render: function() {
    return (
      <div className="todoListMain">
        <div className="header">
          <form onSubmit={this.addItem}>
            <input placeholder="enter task">
            </input>
            <button type="submit">add</button>
          </form>
        </div>
      </div>
    );
  }
});
```

Our `addItem` event handler/function doesn't do a whole lot right now, but the important thing is that it exists! Next, we'll fix the part where it doesn't do a whole lot.

Populating Our State

Right now, our `TodoList` component's `state` object contains the `items` array. What we need to do is populate this array with the text that you enter into the input field. That means we need a way to access our `input` element from within React. The way we are going to do that is by setting a `ref` attribute (as you saw in Chapter 12) on our `input` element and storing the reference to the HTML element that gets generated.

Inside our `TodoList` component's `render` method, add the following line:

```
render: function() {
    return (
      <div className="todoListMain">
        <div className="header">
          <form onSubmit={this.addItem}>
            <input ref={(a) => this._inputElement = a}
                   placeholder="enter task">
            </input>
            <button type="submit">add</button>
          </form>
        </div>
      </div>
    );
  }
```

When this highlighted code runs, which is immediately after this component mounts, the `_inputElement` property will store a reference to the generated `input` element. Now that we have done this, we can treat this element like we would any DOM element we might have found using `querySelector` or equivalent function in the non-React world. What we are going to do next is populate our `items` array!

Go ahead and modify the `addItem` method by adding the following lines:

```
addItem: function(e) {
  var itemArray = this.state.items;

  itemArray.push(
    {
      text: this._inputElement.value,
      key: Date.now()
    }
  );

  this.setState({
    items: itemArray
  });

  e.preventDefault();
}
```

This looks like a lot of code you just added, but all we are doing here is putting into JavaScript our earlier stated goal of populating our `items` array with text from our input field. Let's walk through this code in greater detail.

The first thing we do is create an array called `itemArray` that stores a reference to our `state` object's `items` property:

```
var itemArray = this.state.items;
```

Once we have this array, we add to it our recently submitted text entry from our `input` element:

```
itemArray.push(
  {
    text: this._inputElement.value,
    key: Date.now()
  }
);
```

Notice that we aren't *just* adding the text entry from our `input` element. We are instead adding an object made up of the `text` and `key` properties. The `text` property stores our `input` element's text value. The `key` property stores the current time. This sounds like a bizarre thing to do, but as you recall from Chapter 9, the goal is to have this `key` value be unique for every entry that gets submitted. This is important because (spoiler alert!) we will be using the data in this array to eventually generate some UI elements. This key value is what React will use to uniquely identify each generated UI element, so by generating the key using `Date.now()`, we ensure a certain level of uniqueness. Because this is an important (yet easy to overlook) detail, we will revisit all of this again in a few moments.

Anyway, getting back on track, once we are done with the `itemArray`, all that remains is to set our `state` object's `items` property to it:

```
this.setState({
  items: itemArray
});
```

Almost done here! The last thing we do in this method is the following:

```
e.preventDefault();
```

The `preventDefault` method ensures we override the default **onSubmit** event. The reason we do this is a bit obscure, but it is to ensure the following: all we want to do when we submit the form is call the `addItem` method. If we didn't stop the default behavior, our app will correctly call `addItem` as desired when we submit the form. **It will also trigger our browser's default POST behavior**—which we definitely don't want. By stopping the **onSubmit** event from performing the *default* behavior, we get our *desired* behavior of calling the `addItem` method without any of the unwanted side effects like an unnecessary POST action that might refresh your page.

Displaying the Tasks

We are almost done here! The last-ish thing we are going to do is visualize the tasks that currently live inside our `state` object's `items` array. This is going to involve creating a whole new component called `TodoItems`, passing around some props, using the `map` function, and doing other awesome andrenaline-inducing things (Figure 14-6).

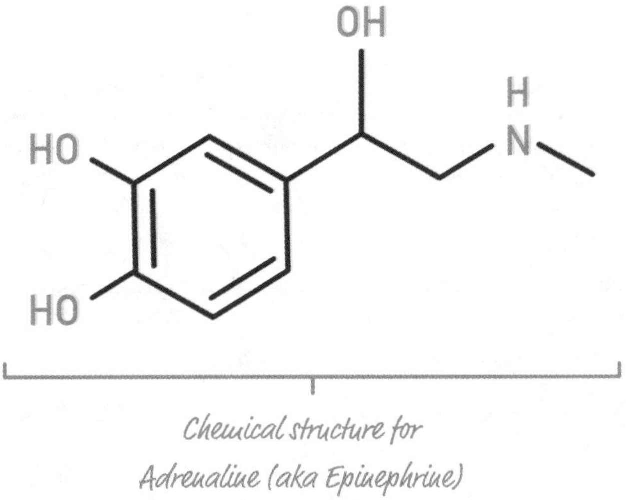

Chemical structure for Adrenaline (aka Epinephrine)

Figure 14-6   Adrenaline!

Anyway, the first thing we are going to do is define our `TodoItems` component. In your code, just above where you have the `TodoList` component defined, go ahead and add the following in:

```
var TodoItems = React.createClass({
  render: function() {

  }
});
```

There is nothing going on right now, but that's OK.

Next, what we are going to do is call this component from inside the `TodoList` component's `render` method. Not only that, we are going to specify a prop and pass in our `TodoList` component's state object that contains our `items` array. Doing all of this is really simple, so go ahead and add the following highlighted line to your `TodoList` component's `render` method:

```
render: function() {
  return (
    <div className="todoListMain">
      <div className="header">
        <form onSubmit={this.addItem}>
```

```
            <input ref={(a) => this._inputElement = a}
                   placeholder="enter task">
            </input>
            <button type="submit">add</button>
          </form>
        </div>
        <TodoItems entries={this.state.items}/>
      </div>
    );
}
```

All we did here is instantiate our `TodoItems` component and pass in our `items` state property to a prop called **entries**. At this point, if you run our app in the browser, nothing visible will happen. Our `TodoItems` component is ready to render, and it has access to all of the tasks that were submitted. The only problem is that it doesn't really do anything with all of that, but we are going to fix that up next.

Getting back to our `TodoItems` component, the first thing we are going to do is create a new variable to store our passed in array of tasks. To do that, add the following highlighted line:

```
var TodoItems = React.createClass({
  render: function() {
    var todoEntries = this.props.entries;


  }
});
```

We just added a variable called `todoEntries`, and it stores the value from the `entries` prop that we passed in based on the `TodoList` component's `this.state.items` value. Sweet! Now, our `todoEntries` variable stores an array containing a bunch of objects that each store a task and a key. All that remains is to create the HTML elements that will be used to display our data.

In the first step towards accomplishing that, add the following highlighted lines of code to create the `li` elements:

```
var TodoItems = React.createClass({
  render: function() {
    var todoEntries = this.props.entries;

    function createTasks(item) {
      return <li key={item.key}>{item.text}</li>
    }

    var listItems = todoEntries.map(createTasks);
  }
});
```

We are using the `map` function to iterate every item inside `todoEntries` and call the `createTasks` function to create a list element for each entry:

```
function createTasks(item) {
  return <li key={item.key}>{item.text}</li>
}
```

To reiterate a point we made earlier, since these list elements are dynamically created, we need to help React keep track of them by specifying the `key` attribute and giving each a unique value. We already solved this part of the problem when we stored our tasks initially, as you recall:

```
itemArray.push(
  {
    text: this._inputElement.value,
    key: Date.now()
  }
);
```

Because of our earlier planning, we take the easy street right now by assigning our `key` attribute the `item.key` value that each item in our `todoEntries` array already contains. Our list element's visible content is simply the text value stored by `item.text`. There is no extra explanation needed for how we use that one. Quite refreshing, isn't it?

Putting all of this together, this collection of list elements is fully processed and stored by our `listItems` variable. All that remains at this point is to go from list elements inside an array to list elements rendered on the screen. To accomplish that, go ahead and add the following highlighted lines:

```
var TodoItems = React.createClass({
  render: function() {
    var todoEntries = this.props.entries;

    function createTasks(item) {
      return <li key={item.key}>{item.text}</li>
    }

    var listItems = todoEntries.map(createTasks);

    return (
      <ul className="theList">
        {listItems}
      </ul>
    );
  }
});
```

What we are doing is returning an `ul` element whose contents are the list elements stored by `listItems`. After you've added this, save your document and preview your app. You'll see something that looks like Figure 14-7 after entering a few tasks.

Figure 14-7   List element for the list items.

Our app works! Every task you submit shows up in its own list item. Take a few deep breaths and relax for a few moments. This is awesome progress, and all we have left are a few little things here and there that need to be wrapped up.

Adding the Finishing Touches

We are almost done here! First, what we have right now doesn't look exactly like the example we started out with. Our list of tasks looks a bit plain, but that can be fixed with some CSS magic. Inside your `style` block, add the following style rules just below where your existing style rules live:

```
.todoListMain .theList {
  list-style: none;
  padding-left: 0;
  width: 255px;
}


.todoListMain .theList li {
  color: #333;
  background-color: rgba(255,255,255,.5);
  padding: 15px;
  margin-bottom: 15px;
  border-radius: 5px;
}
```

If you preview your app now, you'll see that the entered tasks look exactly as you expected them to:

Next, have you noticed that whatever you enter into the input field doesn't go away after you submit the form? You have to manually clear out the field each time after submitting a task...like an animal! That is annoying, but the fix for it is quite simple. Inside our `TodoList` component's `addItem` method, add the following highlighted line:

```
addItem: function(e) {
  var itemArray = this.state.items;

  itemArray.push(
    {
      text: this._inputElement.value,
      key: Date.now()
    }
  );

  this.setState({
    items: itemArray
  });

  this._inputElement.value = "";

  e.preventDefault();
}
```

All we are doing here is clearing our `input` element's `value` property when the form is submitted and the `addItem` method gets called. This ensures that we no longer have to manually clear out our input field between each task we would like to submit. Simple bimple!

Conclusion

Our Todo app is pretty simple in what it does, but by building it from scratch, we covered almost every little interesting detail React brings to the table. More importantly, we created an example that shows how the various concepts we learned individually play together. That is actually the important detail. Now, here is a quick question for you: does everything we've done in this chapter make sense?

If everything we've done in this chapter makes sense then you are in good shape to tell your friends and family that you are close to mastering React! If there are areas that you find confusing, I suggest you go back and re-read the chapters which address your confusion.

15

Setting Up Your React Development Environment

The last major React-related topic we look at is less about React and more about setting up your development environment to build a React app. Up until now, we've been building our React apps by including a few script files:

```
<script src="https://unpkg.com/react@15.3.2/dist/react.js"></script>
<script src="https://unpkg.com/react-dom@15.3.2/dist/react-dom.js"></script>
<script src="https://cdnjs.cloudflare.com/ajax/libs/babel-core/5.8.23/browser.min
.js"></script>
```

These script files not only loaded the React libraries, but they also loaded Babel to help our browser do what needs to be done when it encountered bizarre things like JSX (see Figure 15-1).

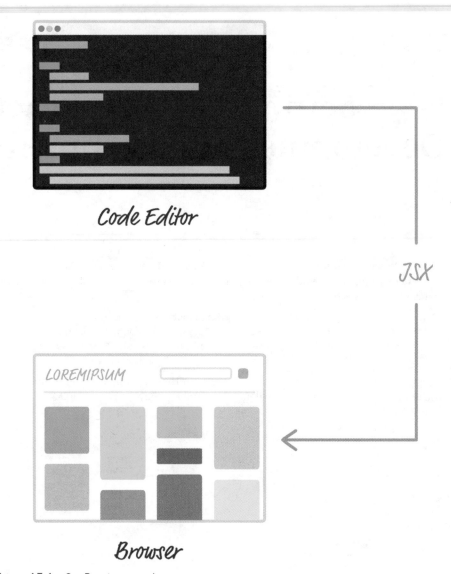

Code Editor

JSX

Browser

Figure 15-1   Our React approach.

To review what we mentioned earlier when talking about this approach, the downside is performance. As part of your browser doing all of the page-loading related things it normally does, it is also responsible for turning your JSX into actual JavaScript. That JSX to JavaScript conversion is a time-consuming process that is fine during development. It isn't fine if every user of your app has to pay that performance penalty.

The solution is to set up your development environment where your JSX to JS conversion is handled prior to the user loading the page (see Figure 15-2).

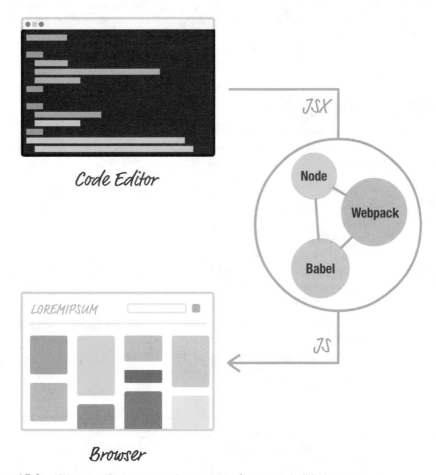

Figure 15-2   JSX to JavaScript conversion as part of your app building process.

With this solution, your browser is loading your app and dealing with an already converted (and potentially optimized) JavaScript file. Good stuff, right? Now, the only reason why we delayed talking about all of this until now is for *simplicity*. Learning React is difficult enough. Adding the complexity of build tools and setting up your environment as part of learning React is just not cool. Now that you have a solid grasp of everything React does, it's time to change that with this chapter.

In the following sections, we look at one way to set up your development environment using a combination of Node, Babel, and webpack. If all of this sounds bizarre to you, don't worry. You'll be on a first name basis with all of these tools by the end of it.

> ### Note: Things May Change
>
> Build tools and their dependencies change all the time. That is great news for us, but it makes publishing information about it a challenge! This chapter contains the latest information based on current (aka when this was written!) best-practices, but this information may change. If you find that some tools and instructions aren't working they way they are described, please check out the (more frequently updated) online version of this article at the following location: https://www.kirupa.com/react/setting_up_react_environment.htm

Meet the Tools

Ok, it is time to move further away from generalities (and sweet diagrams). It is time to get serious—er. It is time to meet the tools that we are going to be relying on to properly set up our development environment.

Node.js

For the longest time, JavaScript was something you wrote to primarily have things happen in your browser. Node.js changes all of this. Node.js allows you to use JavaScript to create applications that run on the server and have access to APIs and system resources that your browser couldn't even dream of. It is basically a full-fledged application development runtime whose apps (instead of being written in Java, C#, C++, etc.) are built and run entirely on JavaScript.

For our purposes, we are going to be relying on Node.js (well, the Node Package Manager, aka NPM) to manage dependencies and tie together the steps needed to go from JSX to JavaScript. Think of Node.js as the glue that makes our development environment work.

Babel

This one should be familiar to us! Simply put, Babel is a JavaScript transpiler. It turns your JavaScript into...um...JavaScript. That sounds really bizarre, so let me clarify. If you are using the latest JavaScript features, older browsers might not know what to do when they encounter a new function or property. If you are writing JSX, well...no browser will know what to do with that!

What Babel does is take your new-fangled JS or JSX and turn into a form of JS that most browsers can understand. We've been using its in-browser version to transform our JSX into JavaScript all this time. In a few moments, you'll see how we can integrate Babel as part of our build process to generate an actual browser-readable JS file from our JSX.

webpack

The last tool we will be relying on is webpack. It is known as a module bundler. Putting the fancy title aside, a lot of the frameworks and libraries your app includes have a lot of dependencies where different parts of the functionality you rely on might only be a subset of larger components.

You probably don't want all of that unnecessary code, and tools like webpack play an important role to enable you to only include the relevant code needed to have your app work. They often bundle all of the relevant code (even if it comes from various sources) into a single file (see Figure 15-3).

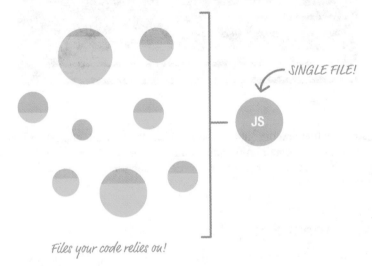

Figure 15-3   Files packed into a single file.

We'll be relying on webpack to bundle up the relevant parts of the React library, our JSX files, and any additional JavaScript into a single file. This also extends to CSS (LESS/SASS) files and other types of assets your app uses, but we'll focus on just the JavaScript side here.

Your Code Editor

No conversation about your development environment can happen without talking about the most important tool in all of this, your code editor (see Figure 15-4).

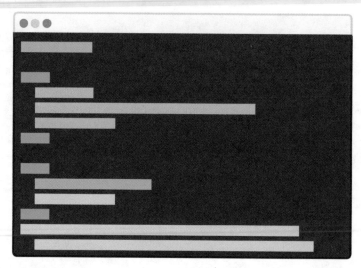

Figure 15-4   Your code editor.

It doesn't matter whether you use Sublime, Atom, VisualStudio Code, TextMate, Coda, or any other tool. You will spend some non-trivial amount of time in your code editor not just to build your React app but to also configure the various configuration files that Node, Babel, and WebPack need.

It Is Environment Setup Time!

At this point, you should have a vague idea of what we are trying to do...the dream we are trying to achieve! We even looked at the various tools that will play a role in making this dream a reality. Now, it is time for the hard work to actually make everything happen.

Setting up our Initial Project Structure

The first thing we are going to do is set up our project. Go to your Desktop and create a new folder called **MyTotallyAwesomeApp**. Inside this folder, create two more folders called **dev** and **output**. Your folder arrangement will look a little bit like Figure 15-5.

Figure 15-5   Our current folder arrangement.

What we are doing here is pretty simple. Inside our **dev** folder, we will place all of our unoptimized and unconverted JSX, JavaScript, and other script-related content. In other words, this is where the code you are writing and actively working on will live. Inside our **output** folder, we will place the result of running our various build tools on the script files found inside the **dev** folder. This is where Babel will convert all of our JSX files into JS. This is also where webpack will resolve any dependencies between our script files, and place all of the important script content into a single JavaScript file.

The next thing we are going to do is create the HTML file that we will point our browser to. Inside the **MyTotallyAwesomeApp** folder, use your code editor to create a new HTML file called **index.html** with the following contents:

```html
<!DOCTYPE html>
<html>

<head>
  <title>React! React! React!</title>
</head>

<body>
  <div id="container"></div>

  <script src="output/myCode.js"></script>
</body>

</html>
```

Be sure to save your file after adding this content in. Now, speaking of the content, our markup is pretty simple. Our document's body is just an empty `div` element with an `id` value of **container** and a `script` tag that points to the final JavaScript file (**myCode.js**) that will get generated inside the **output** folder:

```
<script src="output/myCode.js"></script>
```

Besides those two things, our HTML file doesn't have a whole lot going for it. If we had to visualize the relationship of everything right now, it looks a bit like Figure 15-6.

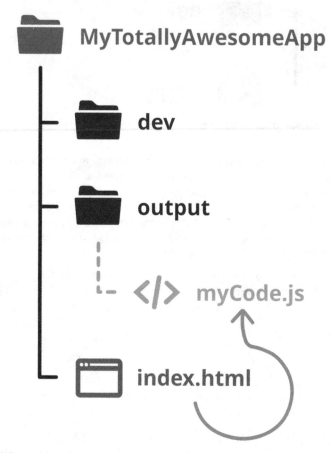

Figure 15-6   What your current project structure looks like.

I've dotted the line to the **myCode.js** file in our **output** folder because that file doesn't exist there yet. We are pointing to something in our HTML that currently is non-existent, but that won't stay that way for long.

Installing and Initializing Node.js

Our next step is to install Node.js. Visit the Node.js site (https://nodejs.org/) to install the version that is appropriate for your operating system (see Figure 15-7).

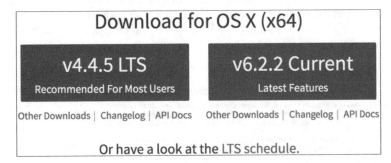

Figure 15-7   The download buttons on the Node.js site.

I tend to always install the latest version, so you should go with that as well. The download and installation procedure isn't particularly exciting. Once you have Node.js installed, test to make sure it is truly installed by launching the Terminal (on Mac), Command Prompt (on Windows), or equivalent tool of choice and typing in the following and pressing Enter:

```
node -v
```

If everything worked out properly, you will see a version number displayed that typically corresponds to the version of Node.js you just installed. If you are getting an error for whatever reason, follow the troubleshooting steps listed here (https://github.com/npm/npm/wiki/Troubleshooting).

Next, we are going to initialize Node.js on our **MyTotallyAwesomeApp** folder. To do this, first navigate to the **MyTotallyAwesomeApp** folder using your Terminal or Command Prompt. On OS X, this will look like Figure 15-8.

Figure 15-8   Navigate to the MyTotallyAwesomeApp folder.

Now, go ahead and initialize Node.js by entering the following:

```
npm init
```

This will kick off a series of questions that will help set up Node.js on our project. The first question will ask you to specify your project name. Hitting Enter will allow you to specify the default value that has already been selected for you. That is all great, but the default name is our project folder, which is **MyTotallyAwesomeApp**. If you hit Enter, because it contains capital letters, it will throw an error (see Figure 15-9).

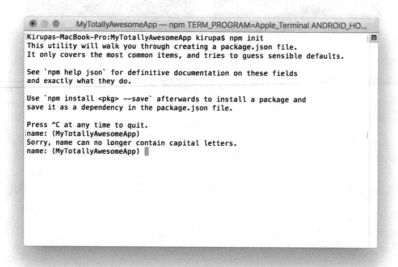

Figure 15-9   Our project folder name includes capital letters, triggering an error.

Go ahead and enter the lowercase version of the name, **mytotallyawesomeapp**. Once you've done that, press Enter. For the remaining questions, just hit Enter to accept all the default values. The end result of all of this is a new file called **package.json** that will be created in your **MyTotallyAwesomeApp** folder (see Figure 15-10).

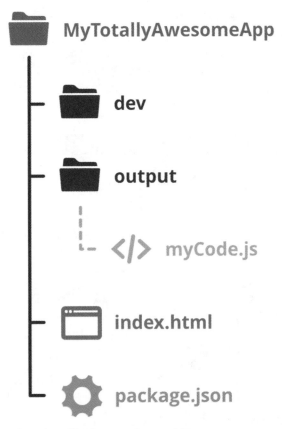

Figure 15-10   The package.json file shows up in your folder.

If you open the contents of **package.json** in your code editor, you'll see something that looks similar to the following:

```
{
  "name": "mytotallyawesomeapp",
  "version": "1.0.0",
  "description": "",
  "main": "index.js",
  "scripts": {
    "test": "echo \"Error: no test specified\" && exit 1"
  },
  "author": "",
  "license": "ISC"
}
```

Don't worry too much about the contents of this file, but just know that one of the results of you calling npm init is that you have a **package.json** file created with some weird properties and values that Node.js totally knows what to do with.

Installing the React Dependencies

What we are going to do next is install our React dependencies so that we can use the React and React DOM libraries in our code. If you are coming from a pure web development background, this is going to sound strange. Just bear with me on this.

In your Terminal or Command Prompt, enter the following to install our React dependencies:

```
npm install react react-dom --save
```

Once you Enter this, a lot of weird stuff will show up on your screen. You may even see a bunch of warnings, but they should be safe to ignore. What is happening is that the React and React-DOM libraries (and stuff that they depend on) is getting downloaded from a giant repository of Node.js packages found here: https://www.npmjs.com/

If you take a look at your **MyTotallyAwesomeApp** folder, you'll see a folder called **node_modules**. Inside that folder, you'll see a bunch of various modules (aka what Node.js calls what we mere mortals just call libraries). Let's update our visualization of our current file/folder structure to look like Figure 15-11.

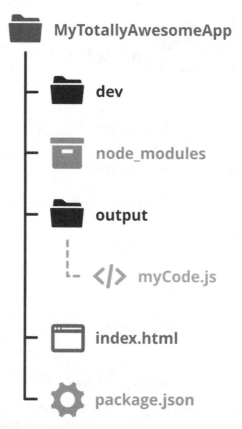

Figure 15-11   The updated folder structure.

The list of modules you see right now is just the beginning. We'll be adding a few more by the time you reach the end of this, so don't get too attached the number of items you see inside our **node_modules** folder :P

Adding our JSX File

Things are about to get (more!) interesting. Now that we've told Node.js all about our interest in React, we are one step closer towards building a React app. We are going to further enter these waters by adding a JSX file that is a modified version of the example we saw in Chapter 3 when looking at Components.

Inside our **dev** folder, using the code editor, create a file called **index.jsx** with the following code as its contents:

```
import React from "react";
import ReactDOM from "react-dom";

var HelloWorld = React.createClass({
  render: function() {
    return (
      <p>Hello, {this.props.greetTarget}!</p>
    );
  }
});

ReactDOM.render(
  <div>
    <HelloWorld greetTarget="Batman"/>
    <HelloWorld greetTarget="Iron Man"/>
    <HelloWorld greetTarget="Nicolas Cage"/>
    <HelloWorld greetTarget="Mega Man"/>
    <HelloWorld greetTarget="Bono"/>
    <HelloWorld greetTarget="Catwoman"/>
  </div>,
  document.querySelector("#container")
);
```

Notice that the bulk of the JSX we added is pretty much unmodified from what we had earlier. The only difference is that what used to be `script` references for getting the React and React DOM libraries into our app has now been replaced with `import` statements pointing to our **react** and **react-dom** Node.js packages we added a few moments ago:

```
import React from "react";
import ReactDOM from "react-dom";
```

Now, you are probably eagerly wondering when we can build our app and get it all working in our browser. Well, there are still a few more steps left. Figure 15-12 shows what the current visualization of our project looks like.

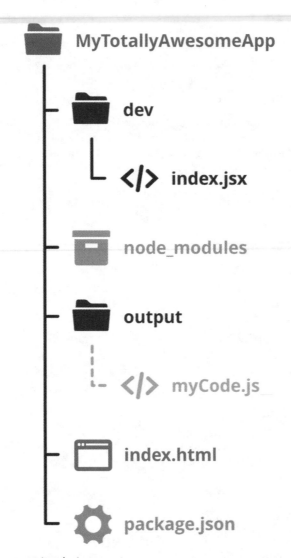

Figure 15-12   The current project.

Our **index.html** file is looking for code from the **myCode.js** file which still doesn't exist. We added our JSX file, but we know that our browser doesn't know what to do with JSX. We need to go from **index.jsx** in our **dev** folder to **myCode.js** in the **output** folder. Guess what we are going to do next?

Going from JSX to JavaScript

The missing step right now is turning our JSX into JavaScript that our browser can understand. This involves both webpack and Babel, and we are going to configure both of them to make this all work.

Setting up webpack

Since we are in Node.js territory and both webpack and Babel exist as Node packages, we need to install them both just like we installed the React-related packages.

To install webpack, enter the following in your Terminal / Command Prompt:

```
npm install webpack --save
```

This will take a few moments while the webpack package (and its large list of dependencies) gets downloaded and placed into our **node_modules** folder. After you've done this, we need to add a configuration file to specify how webpack will work with our current project. Using your code editor, add a file called **webpack.config.js** inside our **MyTotallyAwesomeApp** folder (see Figure 15-13).

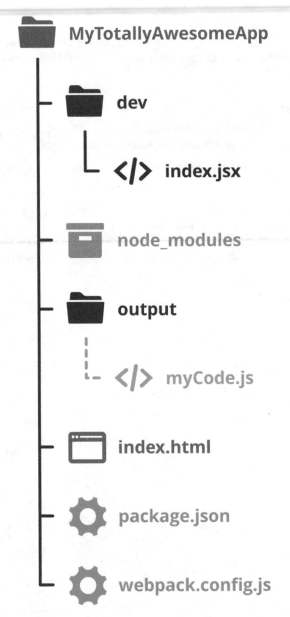

Figure 15-13   Adding webpack.config.js.

Inside this file, we will specify a bunch of JavaScript properties to define where our original, unmodified source files live and where to output the final source files. Go ahead and add the following JavaScript into webpack.config.js:

```
var webpack = require("webpack");
var path = require("path");

var DEV = path.resolve(__dirname, "dev");
var OUTPUT = path.resolve(__dirname, "output");

var config = {
  entry: DEV + "/index.jsx",
  output: {
    path: OUTPUT,
    filename: "myCode.js"
  }
};
```

```
module.exports = config;
```

Take a few moments to see what this code is doing. We defined two variables called DEV and OUTPUT that refer to folders of the same name in our project. Inside the config object, we have two properties called entry and output that use our DEV and OUTPUT variables to help map our **index.jsx** file to become **myCode.js**.

Setting up Babel

The last piece in our current setup is to transform our **index.jsx** file to become regular JavaScript in the form of **myCode.js**. This is where Babel comes in. To install Babel, let's go back to our trusty Terminal / Command Prompt and enter the following Node.js command:

```
npm install babel-loader babel-preset-es2015 babel-preset-react --save
```

With this command, we install the **babel-loader**, **babel-preset-es2015**, and **babel-preset-react** packages. Now we need to configure Babel to work with our project. This is a two-step process.

The first step is to specify which Babel presets we want to use. There are several ways of doing this, but my preferred way is to modify **package.json** and add the following highlighted content:

```
{
  "name": "mytotallyawesomeapp",
  "version": "1.0.0",
  "description": "",
  "main": "index.js",
  "scripts": {
    "test": "echo \"Error: no test specified\" && exit 1"
  },
  "author": "",
  "license": "ISC",
  "dependencies": {
    "babel-loader": "^6.2.4",
```

```
    "babel-preset-es2015": "^6.9.0",
    "babel-preset-react": "^6.5.0",
    "react": "^15.1.0",
    "react-dom": "^15.1.0",
    "webpack": "^1.13.1"
  },
  "babel": {
    "presets": [
      "es2015",
      "react"
    ]
  }
}
```

In the highlighted lines, we specify our `babel` object and specify the **es2015** and **react** preset values.

The second step is to tell webpack about Babel. In our **webpack.config.js** file, go ahead and add the following highlighted lines:

```
var webpack = require("webpack");
var path = require("path");

var DEV = path.resolve(__dirname, "Dev");
var OUTPUT = path.resolve(__dirname, "output");

var config = {
  entry: DEV + "/index.jsx",
  output: {
    path: OUTPUT,
    filename: "myCode.js"
  },
  module: {
    loaders: [{
        include: DEV,
        loader: "babel",
    }]
  }
};

module.exports = config;
```

We added the module and loaders objects that tell webpack to pass the **index.jsx** file defined in our entry property to turn into JavaScript through Babel. With this change, we've pretty much gotten our development environment setup for building a React app.

Building and Testing Our App

The last (and hopefully most satisfying) step in all of this is building our app and having the end-to-end workflow work. To build our app, what you type varies on whether you are on the Terminal or on the Command Prompt.

For the Terminal on the Mac, enter the following:

```
./node_modules/.bin/webpack
```

In the Command Prompt on Windows, enter this instead:

```
node_modules\.bin\webpack.cmd
```

This command runs webpack and does all the things we've specified in our **webpack.config.js** and **package.json** configuration files. Your output in your Terminal / Command Prompt will look something like Figure 15-14.

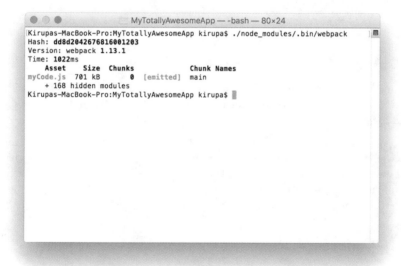

Figure 15-14   The webpack output.

Besides seeing something that vaguely looks like a successful build displayed in cryptic text form, go to your **MyTotallyAwesomeApp** folder. Open your **index.html** file in your browser. If everything was set up properly, you'll see our simple React app displaying (see Figure 15-15).

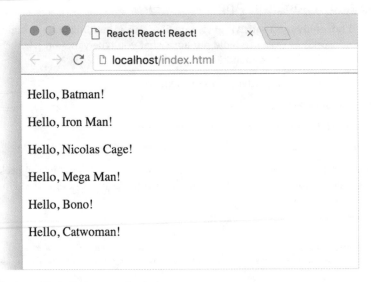

Figure 15-15   The simple React app displaying.

If you venture into the **Output** folder and look at **myCode.js**, you'll see a fairly hefty (~700Kb) file with a lot of JavaScript made up of the relevant React, ReactDOM, and your app code all organized there.

From this point, you can build your app, add new assets, and make the typical changes you normally would. The only difference between what we had been doing throughout this book and what we are doing now is simple—what your browser cares about is generated for you by the various build tools and packager. Your browser is no longer taking all of this React JSX/ES6/etc. stuff and converting it into normal HTML/CSS/JS on the fly during page load.

Conclusion

Well...that just happened! In the preceding many sections, we followed a bunch of bizarre and incomprehensible steps to get our build environment set up to build our React app. What we've seen is just a very small part of everything you can do when you put Node, Babel, and webpack together. The unfortunate thing is that covering all of that goes well beyond the scope of learning React, but if you are interested in this, you should definitely invest time in learning the ins and outs of all of these build tools. There are a lot of cool things you can do.

For more information on those cool things, check out the following links:

- Babel: https://babeljs.io/
- npm Documentation: https://docs.npmjs.com/
- webpack module bundler: https://webpack.github.io/
- React Tooling Integration: https://facebook.github.io/react/docs/tooling-integration.html
- Bower: https://bower.io/

16

The End

So...here we are. After 15 chapters, we've covered a lot of ground when it comes to learning how to use React to build cool things. A while ago, we started off by discussing the problems associated with building complex UIs and how React was going to make that a breeze. Hopefully in the chapters since, you got a really good idea of how you can use React to accomplish this.

While we may be done with the formal content in this book, this doesn't mean that our interaction is over. If you ever have any questions or run into any issues working with React, I'd like to hear from you. The easiest way to contact me is by posting on the forums at http://forum.kirupa.com, but you can also ping me via Twitter (@kirupa) or send me an e-mail (kirupa@kirupa.com). I'll do my best to respond to you as quickly as I can.

See you all next time!

Cheers,

Kirupa ☺

Index

T

Addison-Wesley Learning Series

Visit **informit.com/learningseries** for a complete list of available publications.

The **Addison-Wesley Learning Series** is a collection of hands-on programming guides that help you quickly learn a new technology or language so you can apply what you've learned right away.

Each title comes with sample code for the application or applications built in the text. This code is fully annotated and can be reused in your own projects with no strings attached. Many chapters end with a series of exercises to encourage you to reexamine what you have just learned, and to tweak or adjust the code as a way of learning.

Titles in this series take a simple approach: they get you going right away and leave you with the ability to walk off and build your own application and apply the language or technology to whatever you are working on.

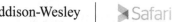

REGISTER YOUR PRODUCT at informit.com/register
Access Additional Benefits and SAVE 35% on Your Next Purchase

- Download available product updates.

- Access bonus material when applicable.

- Receive exclusive offers on new editions and related products.
  (Just check the box to hear from us when setting up your account.)

- Get a coupon for 35% for your next purchase, valid for 30 days. Your code will
  be available in your InformIT cart. (You will also find it in the Manage Codes
  section of your account page.)

Registration benefits vary by product. Benefits will be listed on your account page
under Registered Products.

InformIT.com–The Trusted Technology Learning Source

InformIT is the online home of information technology brands at Pearson, the world's foremost
education company. At InformIT.com you can

- Shop our books, eBooks, software, and video training.
- Take advantage of our special offers and promotions (informit.com/promotions).
- Sign up for special offers and content newsletters (informit.com/newsletters).
- Read free articles and blogs by information technology experts.
- Access thousands of free chapters and video lessons.

Connect with InformIT–Visit informit.com/community
Learn about InformIT community events and programs.

informIT.com
the trusted technology learning source

Addison-Wesley · Cisco Press · IBM Press · Microsoft Press · Pearson IT Certification · Prentice Hall · Que · Sams · VMware Press

ALWAYS LEARNING   PEARSON

Accessing the Free Web Edition

Your purchase of this book in any format includes access to the corresponding Web Edition, which provides several special online-only features:

- The complete text of the book

- Bonus material on animating content with React Motion and making Ajax/server-related calls

- Updates and corrections as they become available

The Web Edition can be viewed on all types of computers and mobile devices with any modern web browser that supports HTML5.

To get access to the *Learning React* Web Edition all you need to do is register this book:

1. Go to www.informit.com/register

2. Sign in or create a new account.

3. Enter ISBN: **9780134546315**

4. Answer the questions as proof of purchase.

5. The Web Edition will appear under the Digital Purchases tab on your Account page. Click the Launch link to access the product.